Nancy MacDonell has written about fashion and style for *The New York Times, Elle,* British *Vogue, NYLON,* and other publications. She was born in Montreal and lives in New York City.

ALSO BY NANCY MACDONELL

*THE CLASSIC TEN: THE TRUE STORY OF THE LITTLE BLACK DRESS
AND NINE OTHER FASHION FAVORITES*

IN THE KNOW

THE CLASSIC GUIDE TO BEING
CULTURED AND COOL

NANCY MACDONELL

PENGUIN BOOKS

PENGUIN BOOKS

Published by the Penguin Group

Penguin Group (USA) Inc., 375 Hudson Street, New York, New York 10014, U.S.A.
Penguin Group (Canada), 90 Eglinton Avenue East, Suite 700, Toronto, Ontario, Canada M4P 2Y3
  (a division of Pearson Penguin Canada Inc.)
Penguin Books Ltd, 80 Strand, London WC2R 0RL, England
Penguin Ireland, 25 St Stephen's Green, Dublin 2, Ireland (a division of Penguin Books Ltd)
Penguin Group (Australia), 250 Camberwell Road, Camberwell, Victoria 3124, Australia
  (a division of Pearson Australia Group Pty Ltd)
Penguin Books India Pvt Ltd, 11 Community Centre, Panchsheel Park, New Delhi – 110 017, India
Penguin Group (NZ), 67 Apollo Drive, Rosedale, North Shore 0632, New Zealand
  (a division of Pearson New Zealand Ltd)
Penguin Books (South Africa) (Pty) Ltd, 24 Sturdee Avenue, Rosebank, Johannesburg 2196,
  South Africa

Penguin Books Ltd, Registered Offices:
80 Strand, London WC2R 0RL, England

First published in Penguin Books 2007

10 9 8 7 6 5 4 3 2 1

Photograph credits: p. 10, Andy Warhol with Edie Sedgwick. Courtesy of Burt Glinn and Magnum
Photos; p. 46, Cindy Sherman, Untitled Film Still 21, 1978. Courtesy of the artist and Metro
Pictures; p. 59, Marc Bolan. Corbis; p. 76, Film still from *Jules et Jim*. Corbis; p. 88, Hill House chair
by Charles Rennie Mackintosh. Reproduced by kind permission of the National Trust for Scotland;
p. 89, Eileen Gray E.1027 table. Courtesy of ClassiCon; p. 90, Marcel Breuer's Wassily chair. Bauhaus-
Archiv Berlin. Foto: Fotostudio Bartsch; p. 92, LC/4 Chaise Longue, Le Corbusier, Pierre Jeanneret,
Charlotte Perriand. Available at Cassina USA, 800-770-3568, www.cassinausa.com; p. 94, Alvar
Aalto vase. Courtesy of Iittala; p. 95, Russel Wright, American Modern table service. © MASCA;
p. 97, Ant Chair, designed by Arne Jacobsen for Fritz Hansen; p. 98, Eames lounge chair and ottoman.
Herman Miller, Inc.; p. 100, Macintosh SE. Frog Design, Inc.; p. 102, Juicy Salif juicer. Alessi
S.p.a., Crusinallo, Italy; p. 125, Coco Chanel taken by Man Ray. © 2007 Man Ray Trust/Artists
Rights Society (ARS), NY/ADAGP, Paris; p. 156, Helmut Newton photo of YSL's *le smoking*. © the
Helmut Newton Estate / Maconochie Photography; p. 194, Debbie Harry at the Mudd Club. Allan
Tannenbaum

LIBRARY OF CONGRESS CATALOGING-IN-PUBLICATION DATA
MacDonell, Nancy.
In the know : the classic guide to being cultured and cool / Nancy MacDonell.
p.   cm.
Includes index.
ISBN 978-0-14-311260-0
1. Lifestyles.   2. Fashion—Social aspects.   3. Culture.   4. Conduct of life.   I. Title.
HQ2042.M33   2007
391—dc22   2007012075

Printed in the United States of America
Set in Adobe Garamond · Designed by Sabrina Bowers

FOR EUAN

ACKNOWLEDGMENTS

THOUGH IT'S TRADITIONAL to start with the professionals and then move on to your personal acknowledgments, I'd like to break with convention and begin by thanking my husband, Euan Robertson, who is surely the most patient and understanding man alive. I'm quite certain he had no idea what he was getting into when he agreed to live with a writer, but he handles it admirably. Stéphanie Abou blurs the line between personal and professional, for she's not only a fantastic agent but a good friend. Indeed, everyone at Global Literary Management is a pleasure to work with. Ali Bothwell Mancini, my editor, understood the idea for this book straightaway and made it immeasurably better with her comments and suggestions. I'd also like to thank Brett Kelly, who, though no longer at Penguin, was instrumental in making it a reality; Rebecca Hunt; Carolyn Waldron; Sabrina Bowers and Roseanne Serra in the art department there; and Evan Gaffney, who designed the cover. I'm grateful to everyone who contributed their expertise, a multitalented, multinational group that includes Viia Beaumanis, Michael Bragg, Jason Campbell, Maria Marta Facchinelli, Jenny Feldman, Karen Gettinger, Gentry Lane, Johanna Lenander, Sophie McKinlay of the Design Museum in London,

Scott Meadows, Mark Oldman, Carolyn Ramos, Christine Samuelian, Michael Sheridan, Tanya Wenman Steel, Francesca Syz, and Yvonne Force Villareal. And, finally, thank you to my friends and family for their moral support and encouraging e-mails.

CONTENTS

INTRODUCTION

ONCE, AS I SAT WAITING for a fashion show to start, I overheard two editors discussing the merits of a third. "I don't know if she understands what she's supposed to be doing," the first was saying. "If she doesn't know what a fashion editor does," retorted her companion, "then she doesn't have the taste to be one."

In its own snide, oblique way, this **Diana Vreeland** moment provided a textbook-perfect definition of what it means to be cool. If you're cool—in this case, not too lacking in taste to be a fashion editor—you're privy to arcane knowledge available only to the initiated. If you're not cool—i.e., have no idea what being a fashion editor entails—then you're left out in the cold. Which is fine if you're equipped with the mental equivalent of a woolly sweater. However, if, like the vast majority of people, you're dying to have access to what insiders know—the ones whose knowledge seems somehow glamorous, anyway—then you're out of luck.

Like being thin or rich, being cool is one of those hallmarks that have universal appeal, because they lead to instant admiration. And all of us, no matter our professional achievements or level of emotional security, yearn to be admired. We want to be perceived as polished, knowledgeable, sophisticated, and worldly. We want to wear the right clothes, reference the right films, allude to the right artists. We want to have friends and strangers alike laugh at our witticisms. When we have people over for dinner, we want them to be impressed with our taste in food, wine, books, music, furniture, and anything else their eyes might land on. We want to be asked where we shop, where we spend our evenings, and where we went on our last holiday. We want to hold our own in conversation. We want to be renowned for our exquisite taste. In short, we want to be cool. The problem is, how?

It was this conundrum that inspired *In the Know: The Classic Guide to Being Cultured and Cool*. For while there are thousands of self-help books in the world, offering advice on everything from investing for the future to having better orgasms, not one of them tackles the more esoteric issues that crop up in life. Why is **Jackson Pollock** important? What handbag will get me upgraded at the airport? Who is **Jacques Derrida**, and why do I need to know about him? These are the sorts of questions that *In the Know* tackles.

Cool is maddeningly elusive to define, which is part of its allure. For the purposes of this book, I've thought of it as cultural literacy combined with a refined aesthetic sense. Like any attempt to classify something that defies characterization, however, it's essentially a personal interpretation. What follows is therefore eclectic and highly subjective. *In the Know* isn't a series of all-time greats or best-of lists. People, places, and things that you may consider the epitome of cool have no doubt been left out. It's not intended to replace books on art history or literary criticism or film studies. In the interest of fitting in as much relevant information as possible, I've left out anything too obvious. You don't need me to tell you who David Bowie is or that you should read *The Catcher in the Rye*, for example. And for the most part, I've confined my subject matter to the modern era, which is to say the nineteenth and twentieth centuries, because that's when our ideas of what cool is were formulated. At the other end of the spectrum, with a few exceptions, anything too recent hasn't been included because it's either too early to tell how it will age, or, again, it doesn't need further explanation. To make it easier to trace the connections between chapters and ideas, everyone and everything that has an entry in this book is in boldface. So if you're wondering why Diana Vreeland was referenced in the second paragraph of this introduction or are reading about **Andy Warhol** and want to know more about **Edie Sedgwick**, you can.

However you classify it, cool is a code, and without the key to the code, it remains unknowable. *In the Know* is a key, and I hope it's a useful and entertaining one. Think of it as a crash course in aesthetics without the panic of having to take an exam at the end.

IN THE KNOW

CULTURE

Susan Sontag had the right attitude toward culture. The point, she often said, quoting Goethe, was "to know everything." She never lost her childhood belief that art—in the broadest sense of the word—could be what she described in one of her most famous essays, "Against Interpretation," as incantatory magical." Granted, Sontag was a professional dilettante; forming and voicing opinions was second nature to her. But she began by looking—and reading and listening—and went from there.

That's the idea behind this section: It's intended to give you a road map with which to navigate modern culture. Not everything that could be included is, of course, or this wouldn't be a chapter in a book, it would be a multivolume boxed set that required biannual revisions. Perhaps an outline would be a better way to describe it, one that contains significant figures and works in various genres.

The chapter is divided into broad categories: Literature, Art, Music, Film, Design, and Architecture. Within each of these sections, I've tried to call out the people who, through their work and life, have made a significant contribution to the culture. Those whose influence is so pervasive that it's impossible to contain under one heading—like Sontag—have been grouped together as Cultural Innovators.

TEN CULTURAL INNOVATORS

IT WOULD BE IMPOSSIBLE to talk about modern culture without these thinkers. Some are writers, others are artists or musicians; all transcended their particular field to make a lasting impact on the way we look at the world. The ideas that everyone will have their fifteen minutes of fame and that the medium is the message and that kitsch is commendable wouldn't be in circulation without them.

FRIEDRICH NIETZSCHE (1844-1900)

Though the nineteenth century was an optimistic age, Friedrich Nietzsche took a dim view of it; that's the kind of guy he was (it's also the reason why generation after generation of disaffected teenagers have adopted him as a spiritual godfather). While others were cheered by the seemingly unstoppable progress of science and technology, he regarded it as a time of crisis, interpreting the era's dwindling belief in religion as the start of a widespread nihilism that, if unchecked, would lead in the next century to unimaginably horrible wars. But the philosopher who's famous for asserting that

"God is dead" was no advocate of religion (or any other mass movement). To Nietzsche, the way out of nihilism was through the creative, willful affirmation of life, a conviction that formed the core of his writings.

Despite his atrocious health—he suffered, among other things, from migraines, periods of near-blindness, and severe stomach pains—he could be a prolific writer. In one five-year period in the 1880s, he wrote eight books, including *Beyond Good and Evil, The Twilight of the Idols,* and *Thus Spake Zarathustra,* a novel-cum-polemic that outlines the key tenets of his philosophy and remains his most widely read work. It's also one of his strangest. *Thus Spake Zarathustra* is written in the style of the Gospels and borrows liberally from the Bible, but it's relentlessly antireligion. And because Nietzsche coupled an unwavering belief in the importance of his work with a well-founded fear that no one understood him, its tone varies from the ecstatic to the scathing (his opinion of the common "rabble"—i.e., those who didn't get him—is particularly low).

The book's protagonist is Zarathustra, better known in English as Zoroaster, a Persian prophet of approximately the fifth century B.C. He preaches the doctrine of the will to power, or the fundamental force that drives all life. The only being who has the will to power is the Overman, who accepts no laws except those he makes for himself. The Overman knows true freedom, because he is strong enough to discipline himself. According to Zarathustra, this is no easy matter, because the universe is in constant turmoil. The same events occur over and over again (sort of like *Groundhog Day* ad nauseam), a phenomenon known as eternal recurrence, and only a truly advanced being can accept responsibility for everything he's ever done and continue accepting that endlessly. Zarathustra concludes that the Overman doesn't exist but must be bred.

Though his ideas were later seized on by the Nazis, Nietzsche wasn't anti-Semitic. His sister Elisabeth, however, was so suspicious of Jews that she and her husband attempted to start an Aryan colony in South America, a venture that caused her brother to burst out laughing when he heard about it. But Elisabeth had the last laugh: She was Nietzsche's literary executrix. After his death, she published his work selectively, to advance her own beliefs. It wasn't until the second half of the twentieth century that Nietzsche's reputation was rehabilitated and his influence on modern philosophy acknowledged.

MARTHA GRAHAM (1894–1991)

In the late 1920s, after one of her early performances, Martha Graham was approached backstage by an actress friend. "Martha, dear, how long do you expect to keep up this dreadful dancing?" the woman asked. "As long as I have an audience," Graham replied. The audience, it turned out, wasn't going anywhere. Graham was seventy-five when she took her final bow, and when she died at ninety-six, she was in the midst of choreographing one last ballet.

Between those first "dreadful" performances and her later years as a cultural lion, Graham revolutionized dance. She wasn't the first woman to cast aside her point shoes and dance barefoot, but her willingness to push boundaries put her in a league all her own. Like **Picasso** or **Frank Lloyd Wright**, she made a definitive break with the past to create a completely new form of expression.

Before Graham, dance came in two forms: classical ballet, with its emphasis on formal poses and prescribed ways of moving, and modern dance in the style of Ruth St. Denis (whom Graham studied with) and Isadora Duncan, who gestured and whirled in exotic costumes but were still recognizably graceful. Graham rejected all of that. Instead of soaring through the air, as ballerinas traditionally did, her dancers hugged the ground. Their movements, especially their ferocious pelvic jerks, were spastic and disjunctive. They ran, leapt, trembled, and fell—hard. And they didn't portray swans or sugarplum fairies. Graham tore dance from its aristocratic moorings, creating ballets that commented on politics, war, poverty, intolerance, sex, and other impolite topics. Her heroines, including Clytemnestra, Joan of Arc, and Emily Dickinson, were independent and strong. They could also be monsters: One of her most memorable roles was Medea, in which she symbolically ate her own entrails.

Audiences were often puzzled by Graham's ballets, and sometimes horrified, but never indifferent. Her most enduring work, however, is her most straightforwardly lyrical and uncomplicated.

Appalachian Spring (1944) is a joyful imagining of a pioneer wedding. Aaron Copland wrote the score, and it was originally performed in a spare set designed by Graham's frequent collaborator, the sculptor Isamu Noguchi. Graham played the bride, a role she didn't give up until she was in her sixties. The mother of modern dance found it almost impossible to leave the stage. Even when arthritis had turned her hands into claws and her signature red lipstick and white powder had stiffened into a mask, she lingered on. Even when she no longer danced herself, she kept teaching, telling her students, "Stand up! Keep your backs straight! Remember that this is where the wings grow."

GEORGE BALANCHINE (1904-1983)

To George Balanchine, or Mr. B., as he was known to generations of dancers, all ballet needed to come alive was music. In the more than two hundred works he created, he took what had been an art form that shared a cluttered stage with storytelling, mimed acting, and elaborate sets and distilled it to its purest, most essential form. Even when his company performed in their rehearsal clothes in his signature plotless ballets, his clean, graceful choreography was captivating—so entwined with the score that he spoke of "seeing the music and hearing the dance."

In the first of many coincidences that were to mark his life and career, the foremost creator of ballets in the twentieth century was born on January 22, 1904, the same day that Marius Petipa, the legendary nineteenth-century creator of ballets such as *The Sleeping Beauty,* carped in his journal that he had no successor to take over his life's work. Balanchine was proud of his classical heritage and his debt to his "spiritual father," but his aesthetic was sharpened by the artistic foment thrown up by the Russian Revolution and the rhythm of life in America. Mr. B.'s dancers may have followed in the steps that Petipa had devised, but they had a swiftness and athleticism that would have left the older man breathless.

Balanchine was a teenage ballet student at the Imperial Ballet School when the Revolution broke out, forcing it to close its doors. He took up his studies again a year later, but in the end decamped for Europe, where he met Sergei Diaghilev, who invited the twenty-one-year-old novice to be the principal choreographer for his Ballets Russes (he also suggested that he change his name from Georgi Balanchivadze to something that Europeans would find easier to pronounce). But Diaghilev died suddenly in 1929, and the company was disbanded, leaving Balanchine at loose ends. His next fateful encounter came in 1934, when the American balletomane Lincoln Kirstein persuaded him to come to the United States, where the two would go on to found the School of American Ballet and the New York City Ballet. Balanchine was the master in chief of the City Ballet from its debut performance in 1948 to his death, and it was there that he created some of his most enduring ballets, including *La Valse, Agon, Episodes* (a collaboration with **Martha Graham**), *The Nutcracker,* and a series of works set to music by the avant-garde composer Igor Stravinsky. He also choreographed four Broadway shows and nineteen films; Balanchine may have been a classicist, but he wasn't a snob.

It's sometimes said that Balanchine, who once declared "ballet is a woman," was a better choreographer for women than for men. Though this isn't strictly true, he did make prima ballerinas of several of his female dancers, and married an unprecedented four of them in the process (he had a common-law relationship with a fifth), including City Ballet soloists Maria Tallchief and Tanaquil LeClerq.

SIMONE DE BEAUVOIR (1908-1986) AND JEAN-PAUL SARTRE (1905-1980)

Simone de Beauvoir and Jean-Paul Sartre met in Paris in 1929, while both were studying for the highly competitive *agrégation* examination (a passing grade was necessary to teach in the French school system) in philosophy. Sartre came in first and Beauvoir, who was the youngest person ever to pass the exam, came in second. She was considered the better student by the examiners, but because it was Sartre's second attempt and he was a man, he was awarded the top mark. Given that sort of bias, it's a wonder that it took Beauvoir another twenty years to write her magnum opus, *The Second Sex* (1949). A work of existentialist feminism laced with

Freudian analysis, it was one of the tracts that prodded second-wave feminists such as Betty Friedan into action.

Both Beauvoir and Sartre were proponents of existentialism, which holds that life has no essential meaning and that each existing individual must therefore apply his or her own—necessarily subjective—values to his or her experience. Sartre's novel *Nausea* (1938) is the movement's manifesto (the title comes from the ever-cheerful **Nietzsche**, who used the term to describe the sick feeling that arises when contemplating the mediocrity of existence). But it was the mystique of Beauvoir and Sartre's open relationship that gave existentialism its postwar glamour. By taking the French tradition of public intellectualism and mixing it with carnal license and a disregard for common propriety, they made it sexy to be cerebral.

Sartre's attraction to Beauvoir is understandable. She was good-looking, stylish, and passionate. That his feelings were reciprocated is more perplexing, as he was freakishly short, indifferent to personal hygiene, and incapable of fidelity, which he considered a bourgeois convention. When he suggested that they could each have affairs, so long as they told each other all about them, Beauvoir, who was eager to escape the influence of her suffocating bourgeois family, agreed. Their relationship, a sort of *Dangerous Liaisons* transported to the cafés of midcentury Paris, was to last until Sartre's death.

Rather than conducting independent affairs, the couple preferred to be unfaithful in tandem. Though Beauvoir had relationships with other men, she tended to become involved with the same women Sartre was sleeping with. These were often young, impressionable girls whom the two would take in and adopt (creepily, Beauvoir referred to their ongoing ménage and its shifting cast of characters as the Family, and Sartre actually did legally adopt one of his conquests). It's unclear why Beauvoir put up with all this. In her barely fictionalized accounts of these incestuous hook-ups, *She Came to Stay* (1943) and *The Mandarins* (1955), the Beauvoir characters are pitiable. Whatever her reasoning, neither she nor Sartre were vindicated by their letters, which were published in unedited form only after their deaths. Their voluminous correspondence reveals them to be petty, hypocritical, and contemptuous of pretty much everyone around them, but especially their lovers.

MARSHALL McLUHAN (1911–1980)

Though the phrases he coined or popularized—including "the medium is the message" and the "global village"—are repeated every day, the media scholar Marshall McLuhan didn't think many people understood them, a conviction that was summed up by his cameo appearance in Woody Allen's 1977 film *Annie Hall*. In the film, Alvy Singer (Allen) gets irritated with a man he overhears trying to impress his date by spouting McLuhanisms. He tells the man, who identifies himself as a Columbia University professor and expert on McLuhan, that he doesn't know what he's talking about. To prove his point, Alvy reaches out and pulls McLuhan into the frame. Much to Alvy's satisfaction, McLuhan corrects the professor's analysis, and adds, "You know nothing of my work. How you got to teach a course in anything is totally amazing."

The man who appeared on *Wired* magazine's masthead as "patron saint" was born in Edmonton, Alberta, and spent most of his career at the University of Toronto. His field was English literature, but thanks to his writings on modern media, he became famous as a communications theorist. In books such as *The Gutenberg Galaxy* (1962) and *Understanding Media: The Extensions of Man* (1964), McLuhan held forth on theories that have shaped how media developments such as reality television and the Internet have been written about. Critics he's influenced include Neil Postman, Camille Paglia, and Timothy Leary, who traced the origin of his own famous phrase "turn on, tune in, drop out" to a conversation with McLuhan.

McLuhan posited that all media, regardless of their content, have a profound effect on society, from the way we process information to societal structure, and that the characteristics of each medium are as worthy of study as the messages they convey—hence "the medium is the message," which eventually evolved into "the medium is the massage," reflecting McLuhan's research into how media stimulates, or "massages" the senses. New technologies, in his view, have an especially pronounced impact ("We become what we behold. We shape our tools and thereafter they shape us"). The printing press, for example, was the catalyst for the shift from an oral culture to a visual one, and precipitated the move away from a tribal societal structure to one that was centered on the individual. Though McLuhan's prediction that we were moving back into an oral/tribal society has been questioned, it's where his theory of the global village, which he saw as a period of time rather than a concept, was first outlined. But then, as McLuhan himself said, "I don't explain—I explore."

ANDY WARHOL (1928–1987)

Decades before reality television came to dominate the airwaves and provide endlessly recycled fodder for the supermarket weeklies, Andy Warhol knew where popular culture was heading. "In the future," he predicted, "everyone will be famous for fifteen minutes." (He later joked that "in fifteen minutes everybody will be famous," which also appears to be coming true.) More than any other artist (he was also a filmmaker and publisher) of his generation, Warhol was a one-man cultural conduit, plugged straight into the zeitgeist. It was this insight that gave his work its wide-reaching resonance and put him at the forefront of the **pop art** movement.

Celebrity, whether of a person or a brand, fascinated him. He was obsessed with surfaces and appearances, and repeatedly said that if you wanted to under-

Andy Warhol poses with Edie Sedgwick, the poor little rich girl who became one of his superstars and a latter-day fashion icon.

stand his work, you had only to look at it—there wasn't anything more to it than that. Though that's somewhat disingenuous, there's an element of truth to it. By turning everyday objects like Brillo soap boxes into art, Warhol was both celebrating mass culture and commenting on it, offering an iconography of consumerism that fell into line with his comment that department stores are like museums. His best-known work, his series of celebrity silk screens of gay icons such as Marilyn Monroe, is, Warhol's glibness about superficiality aside, as eloquent a reaction to living in a media-saturated culture as you can imagine.

From making art of mass-produced items, Warhol switched to mass-producing art in 1962, when he opened his studio, the Factory—irony was another concept Warhol pioneered—and hired art workers to churn out prints, paintings, and films under his supervision. The Factory looms large in any study of cool, if only because of the cast of characters that passed through its doors, many of whom were immortalized in Lou Reed's "Walk on the Wild Side": Gerard Malanga, Ultra Violet, Viva, Candy Darling, Paul Morrissey, **Edie Sedgwick**, and Joe D'Alessandro. Warhol promoted them as the new breed of celebrity and cast them in his experimental, often monotonous, sometimes pornographic films.

In 1968, Warhol was shot by a Factory regular named Valerie Solanas, who was the sole member of a group called Society for Cutting Up Men (SCUM). The incident had a profound effect on him: Physically, he never really recovered; creatively, he went into semiretirement. One of his last new projects was the launch of *Interview* magazine in 1973. In it, he took his fascination with fame and money to new heights by having celebrities interview other celebrities.

JACQUES DERRIDA (1930–2004)

If you've come across the term "deconstructed" recently—applied to a dress, a building, or a dinner entrée—you have Jacques Derrida to thank for it. The French philosopher was known as the

> **PRONUNCIATION GUIDE**
>
> **Jacques Derrida:**
> **JHZOCK DAY-ree-da**

father of deconstruction, a school of thought that holds that all writing is a morass of latent contradictions and confusions that, because of the inherent paradoxes of language, even the best-intentioned author cannot foresee or overcome. Though initially intended as a method of analysis for literary, historical, and philosophical texts, deconstruction has been expanded to include art, architecture, music, fashion—pretty much every creative undertaking or social science you can think of is now routinely deconstructed, making it one of the most overused and least understood concepts of the past forty years. The allure of deconstruction, however, is seductive whether you understand it or not; we all know that things are not necessarily what they seem.

Derrida was that improbable phenomenon, a French intellectual who was more popular in the United States than in his own country. To his supporters, his theories were tools with which to challenge the authority of the dead white men of the Western canon—Aristotle, Shakespeare, Sigmund Freud, et al. To his detractors, deconstruction and its partner in crime, relativism (the idea that truth is subjective), undermined the very foundations of Western civilization. But regardless of their views on deconstruction, few would call Derrida an easy read. His long sentences, dense with epigrams and academic jargon, are virtually impenetrable. Even the titles of his works can be difficult. One, an interpretation of James Joyce's *Ulysses,* is called *Ulysses Gramophone: Hear Say Yes in Joyce.*

As an Algerian Jew who grew up in postwar France, Derrida was well aware of the dangers of totalitarianism and rigid ideologies. Against this backdrop, his reluctance to acknowledge commonly accepted authority makes perfect sense (**Nietzsche**, another iconoclast, was one of his main philosophical influences). But his uncompromising position made him enemies. After the death of one of his closest friends and supporters, the Belgian-born Yale University professor Paul de Man, in 1983, it was revealed that de Man had written more than a hundred anti-Semitic articles for a Nazi newspaper in Belgium during the Second World War. Derrida defended de Man, and used deconstructive techniques in an attempt to show that de Man's articles weren't really anti-Semitic. The incident caused a major academic scandal and seriously damaged Derrida's reputation.

Though Derrida's influence waned in the last fifteen years of his life, his place as one of the most influential—and controversial—philosophers of the twentieth century is indisputable.

SUSAN SONTAG (1933–2004)

A self-described "besotted aesthete" and "obsessed moralist," Susan Sontag was the most highly regarded and high-profile American intellectual of her generation, as widely known for her critical brilliance as for her white-streaked dark hair. Her omnivorous curiosity led her to approach culture as an all-you-can-eat buffet, and she tucked into topics as diverse as Albert Camus, rock 'n' roll, photography, and the ballets of **George Balanchine**, analyzing their nuances and finding the connections among them. "When I go to a **Patti Smith** concert, I enjoy, participate, appreciate and am tuned in better because I've read **Nietzsche**. The main reason I read is that I enjoy it. There's no incompatibility between observing the world and being tuned into an electronic, multimedia, multitracked, **McLuhan**ite world and enjoying what can be enjoyed about rock 'n' roll," she wrote. An iconoclast, Sontag didn't shy away from debunking accepted dogma. In an essay titled "Against Interpretation," she even questioned the need for critical analysis, worrying that it interfered with the cathartic power of art. But her most influential piece was one of her earliest, 1964's "Notes on 'Camp.' " In it, she introduced the then-nascent so-bad-it's-good aesthetic that's become a hallmark of contemporary culture, applying it to everything from Aubrey Beardsley's drawings to feather boas, and examining its roots in gay culture. Sontag was herself bisexual, though she rarely referred to her private life in public. She had a long relationship with the photographer Annie Leibovitz.

Along with her critical essays, Sontag wrote fiction; her historical novel, *In America,* won the National Book Award in 2000. She was also a committed political activist who was unafraid to hold maverick opinions. Following the terrorist attacks on the World Trade Center, she asked in an essay in *The New Yorker,* "Where is the acknowledgment that this was not a 'cowardly' attack on 'civilization' or 'liberty' or 'humanity' or 'the free world' but an attack on the world's self-proclaimed superpower, undertaken as a consequence of specific American alliances and actions?" In the resulting firestorm, she was accused of being un-American by both bloggers and mainstream commentators.

Despite her gloom about the direction the world was going in, Sontag was a passionate humanist for whom art had a limitless capacity to inform and delight. A good book, she told *The Paris Review,* "is an education of the heart. It enlarges your sense of human possibility, of what human nature is, of what happens in the world. It's a creator of inwardness."

GERMAINE GREER (B. 1939)

The reliably controversial, always illuminating, occasionally mad Germaine Greer is one of the most important figures in second-wave feminism. Her breakthrough work was *The Female Eunuch* (1970), a revelatory bombshell that prompted a generation of women to look at themselves and their marriages from a radically altered perspective. Greer's thesis was that the traditional nuclear family represses women's sexuality, thus draining them of vitality, individuality, and any capacity for joy. The only way to rectify the situation, she argued, was revolution. She urged women to love their bodies, embrace their sexuality, and give up monogamy. Not surprisingly, *The Female Eunuch* and its unequivocal message of "down with the patriarchy" caused an uproar. Its impact on popular culture was something like that of Darwin's *Origin of Species* divided along gender lines.

The Australian-born Greer appears to relish the attention her provocative statements attract—she's part academic, part performance artist. Like the pre–English gentlewoman Madonna, to whom she's often compared—and whose singing and dancing she deplores, though she confesses to an admiration for her marketing acumen—Greer's larger-than-life personality is her best asset. She's written at length about her life: her sexual encounters (hetero and homo), her abortion, her three-week marriage, and her relationship with her father. This tendency to solipsism has led to criticism that her writing is too self-centered and that she has a tendency to translate her personal experiences into a commentary on those of all women.

Greer's follow-ups to *The Female Eunuch,* which include *Sex and Destiny: The Politics of Human Fertility* (1984), *The Change: Women, Aging and the Menopause* (1992), and *The Whole Woman* (1999) didn't have the groundbreaking effect her first book did, but they sparked controversies of their own. In *The Whole Woman,* for example, she compared female circumcision in the developing world to breast augmentation in the first world, an analogy that led to accusations that she condones the former. But one of Greer's more maddening qualities is that she seems to revel in easy—and misleading—interpretations of her work. In the eyes of many readers, *Daddy, We Hardly Knew You* (1989), her enraged memoir of her distant father, reduced her previous storming against patriarchal injustices to a scorned daughter's hurt, an effect she blithely ignored.

But even in her sixties, doing the conventional thing doesn't interest Greer. In 2005, she was a contestant on the British version of *Big Brother.* She walked off the show after five days, calling the producers "bullies" who ran a "fascist prison." And in 2006, after Steve Irwin, the Aussie crocodile hunter, was killed by a stingray, she described him as "embarrassing" and those who mourned him as "idiots."

PHILIP GLASS (B. 1937)

Like Igor Stravinsky, the radical Russian composer whose score for the ballet *Rite of Spring* prompted fistfights when it was first performed in 1913, Philip Glass doesn't create cozy music. One early review was headlined "Music of Philip Glass Called Sonic Torture." The writer goes on to note that the audience dwindled steadily during the performance, many covering their ears as they fled the auditorium.

But the figurehead for musical minimalism isn't concerned with producing the aural equivalent of a warm bath. His compositions, especially early pieces such as the six-hour-long *Music in 12 Parts* (1974), are demanding, jarring, and aggravating—as well as hypnotic and beautiful. The dozen-plus operas he's written, including *Satyagraha* (1980), about Gandhi, and *The Fall of the House of Usher* (1987), based on the short story by Edgar Allan Poe, are considered some of the best examples of that art form created in the twentieth century. His film work, which ranges from his music for the frenetic, sensory-assaulting *Koyaanisqatsi* (1982), a plotless cinematic collage of modern life, to the quietly lush, Academy Award–nominated score he created for *The Hours* (2002), is equally celebrated.

From the time he was a child, Glass was immersed in music. His father had a record shop and would bring home and listen to disks that didn't sell—everything from jive to Bartók—to try to figure out why no one wanted them. But despite his obvious talent, success eluded Glass in the early part of his career. Throughout the 1970s, he worked as a cabbie and plumber in New York City (he once found himself in the kitchen of astounded *Time* magazine art critic Robert Hughes, who demanded to know what an artist of his caliber was doing installing a dishwasher). It wasn't until *Einstein on the Beach* (1976), a collaboration with the visionary playwright/theater director Robert Wilson, that he reached a wider audience. The allegorical, five-hour-long opera about Albert Einstein's life and theories was a critical smash and went on to tour Europe and North America.

Glass has been canny in choosing his collaborators. Many, including David Bowie, author Doris Lessing, artists Richard Serra and Chuck Close, and Ravi Shankar, are friends, and their various talents and viewpoints have meant that his music is constantly evolving and adapting to new challenges. It's also meant that Glass's work covers an unusually large spectrum, from the experimental fringes to the mainstream, so that his compositions can pop up in some unusual places—like fashion shows. His fourth symphony in 1997, which was inspired by the Bowie album *Heroes* (1977), was used by Marc Jacobs for his fall 2006 runway show.

TEN BOOKS YOU SHOULD READ

THOUGH WE LIVE IN an increasingly visual world, a familiarity with literature is still the badge of a cultivated intellect. You can't really consider yourself well read if you aren't at least on nodding terms—i.e., someone mentions the Fitzgeraldian nature of preppy style, you nod confidently—with the following novels.

MADAME BOVARY (1857), GUSTAVE FLAUBERT (1821-1880)

Gustave Flaubert didn't know what a cottage industry he was launching when he wrote *Madame Bovary*—it's nothing less than the first sex-and-shopping novel. The basic plot is simple, archetypal even: Beautiful, bored Emma Bovary, trapped in an unfulfilling marriage to a provincial dullard, seeks solace in extramarital sex and retail therapy. The worse things get, the more she spends, until her debts

> **PRONUNCIATION GUIDE**
>
> **Gustave Flaubert:**
> **goo-STAHV flow-BEAR**

overwhelm her completely and she kills herself by stuffing a fistful of arsenic into her mouth.

Reading *Madame Bovary* for the first time can be a profoundly depressing experience. Emma's not very likable. Her petit bourgeois life is stultifying; her affairs tawdry and loveless. Her most intense experiences derive from the romance novels she's addicted to. Her life seems devoid of any real feeling. Even her adultery is prompted not by passion but by shopping. Her first affair, which begins with a riding lesson, is spurred on because her husband promises her a new outfit: "The riding-habit decided her," is Flaubert's economic (in all senses of the word) assessment of her priorities. And woven throughout the novel is the suggestion that there is no escape from this meaninglessness, that one can choose either to live in the dreamworld of books (fatal in Emma's case) or be bored literally to death.

But while it's a peerless study of boredom, *Madame Bovary* is never boring. It's all about things and the fascinating minutiae of things: clothes, shoes, furniture, meals, carriages, operas, and balls are all subject to Flaubert's cinematographer's eye. It's an incredibly sensual novel, crammed with oblique sexual references. Emma's husband, for example, is described as "the spike in the buckle of the complicated set of straps that cramped her every step." And the careful reader will find ample evidence of Flaubert's foot fetish: Emma's dainty feet and shoes are noted by all her male admirers.

A century and a half after *Madame Bovary* was published (and its author taken to court for obscenity), our choices aren't nearly so narrow as those that condemned Emma. But the main reason *Madame Bovary* is still relevant is its examination of the yawning emptiness of modern life, an emptiness that, Emma-like, we try to fill with clothes, travel, yoga, macrobiotic diets—anything that fits on a credit card. If Flaubert were writing today, he might have Emma go into debt over Botox injections or breast implants. The number of women who really do this suggests that, despite Flaubert's legendary misogyny, his novel can be interpreted as a feminist cautionary tale. Reader: Emma allows her fantasies to sap the life out of her. Consider yourself forewarned.

But why does Emma have to die? Her death conforms to the requirements of the nineteenth-century novel, which stipulated that any woman who strayed so far from home deserved no better.

But some critics have suggested that Emma was condemned for another, subtler crime. At several points in the novel, she appropriates male clothes and attitudes. She smokes a pipe, wears a waistcoat, downs an entire tumbler of brandy. And she's ravenously sexual—as the carriage ride with her younger lover, during which Flaubert intimates that the two have sex all afternoon, demonstrates. Emma knows who's in charge, and she wants some of their power for herself. She becomes, as the novelist Michèle Roberts writes, "less of a woman and more of a monster. She cannot be allowed to live."

THE PICTURE OF DORIAN GRAY (1890/91), OSCAR WILDE (1854-1900)

"There is no such thing as a moral or immoral book. Books are well written or they are badly written. That is all," drawls Lord Henry Wotton in *The Picture of Dorian Gray,* the gilded-age novel that has served as a primer for nascent bad boys and wannabe rock stars even since it was published. As Oscar Wilde must surely have foreseen—everything the decadent Lord Henry says is a calculated affront to the middle-class values of the time—late-Victorian readers didn't agree. *The Picture of Dorian Gray,* with its hints of drug use, homosexual sex, and other titillating debaucheries, horrified critics and the public alike when it was published in 1890 (a revised, slightly toned-down version came out a year later). It was a spectacular succès de scandale, propelling the author to dizzying heights and then dropping him into an abyss of defamation, ignominy, and prison.

The plot revolves around the usual Faustian bargain: Dorian Gray, a beautiful young man in love with his own good looks, sells his soul in exchange for eternal youth (the novel's set in the late nineteenth century, so Dorian is a gentleman of independent means—today, he'd be an actor). Wilde's brilliant conceit was to add the portrait, which over time shows all the ugliness of Dorian's increasingly dissolute life, which he is led into by Lord Henry. Dorian eventually attempts to destroy the portrait so that no one may see its horrors but succeeds only in destroying himself. When his servants break into the room, they find a hideous old man with a dagger in his heart lying before a painting of a once-again dazzlingly handsome young man.

The hostility that greeted *Dorian Gray* was due in no small part to the novel's homoerotic undertones, and, indeed, rumors of Wilde's sexual orientation had swirled for years. But almost as distasteful to his peers was the novel's bold articulation of the beliefs of the aesthetics movement, of which Wilde was a leading member. The aesthetes, who included Charles Baudelaire, Théophile Gautier, and Joris-Karl Huysmans, held that art should have no other purpose than to provide pleasure—to be beautiful, as Dorian is. This kind of talk sent shudders through the straitlaced Victorian establishment, which believed that art should be a tool of moral enlightenment. But the art-for-art's-sake dogma is one that goes hand-in-hand with self-indulgent sensuality. Just as Dorian is fascinated and inspired by the Huysmans novel *Against Nature,* about an overbred aristocrat who retires to a country villa to engage in elaborate hedonism, so the haute bohemians of the '60s pored over both that and *The Picture of Dorian Gray* (Marianne Faithfull said that at the time, she'd check to see if a man had read *Against Nature* before sleeping with him) for sybaritic how-tos.

Dorian Gray proved Wilde's undoing. In 1895, he was arrested and charged with sodomy, then illegal in Britain. At his trial, the novel was used as evidence against him. He was found guilty and sentenced to two years' imprisonment with hard labor. When he was released, he changed his name and moved to Paris, where he died in 1900, penniless.

THE METAMORPHOSIS (1915), FRANZ KAFKA (1883–1924)

The Metamorphosis begins like a fairy tale gone wrong: "When Gregor Samsa awoke one morning from troubled dreams, he found himself changed into a monstrous insect in his bed." With an opening like that, you know things can only get worse. And do they ever: On discovering Gregor's condition, his horrified family hustles him back into his room so they don't have to look at his revolting new form—even his beloved sister is disgusted by him. Moreover, rather than worrying about Gregor's mysterious transformation, all his family can think of is how it affects them, especially since they'd relied on his salary to provide their comforts. His father is particularly spiteful: When Gregor emerges from his room one day, he hurls apples at him, one of which lodges in Gregor's back and festers.

The next time Gregor ventures out, his family is uncompromising. "We must get rid of it," his sister says. "You just have to put any thought from your mind that it's Gregor. . . . If it was Gregor, he would have long ago seen that it's impossible for human beings to live together with an animal like that, and he would have left of his own free will." Completely rejected, Gregor crawls back to his room to die of neglect, lack of food, and the infected wound in his back. The next morning, the Samsas discover his corpse. Their spirits rise immediately, and they decide they're not doing so badly after all. A walk in the park is suggested, and Gregor is quickly forgotten.

The Metamorphosis has kept literary critics busy for the better part of a century. Is it a commentary on society's treatment of outsiders? An extreme family drama of a son who resented his father's overbearing personality? A warning of the rise of totalitarianism and the banality of terror? Or an early example of Monty Python–style humor? Kafka may have trumped for the last interpretation. In his diary, he notes approvingly that when he read his novella out loud to his friends, they all laughed uproariously. The poster boy for modern angst plays the pitch-black humor dead straight, which is why you never question the veracity of his story. Neither Gregor nor his family, for example, appear particularly shocked by his transformation. In fact, Gregor's initial concern is remarkably pedestrian: He worries that it's going to make him late for work, a reaction that anyone who's ever held down a dead-end job can relate to. It's as though he's aware his situation is what we've come to describe as Kafkaesque—nightmarish, utterly hopeless, and completely absurd. As the twentieth century and its various horrors ground on, it proved to be an influential sensibility: The novelist Milan Kundera traces the absurdities in the work of such pivotal figures as **Federico Fellini** and **Gabriel García Márquez** to Kafka's trailblazing sense of the painfully surreal.

But then Kafka knew what it was to have your destiny determined by a spiteful fate. He died at forty, of tuberculosis. In the last few weeks of his life, the condition of his throat made swallowing too painful for him to eat; like Gregor, he starved to death.

ORLANDO (1928),
VIRGINIA WOOLF (1882-1941)

Virginia Woolf described *Orlando,* a fantastical biography-cum-work-of-fiction, as "a writer's holiday." It is in fact a valentine to the poet Vita Sackville-West, for whom Woolf nourished a fierce passion. It's also Woolf's most playful and funny work, and the pleasure she took in writing it is evident on every page.

Woolf imagines her friend as Orlando, an exceptionally handsome young nobleman at the court of Queen Elizabeth I. He catches the eye of the Queen, woos a feckless Russian princess, and becomes ambassador to Constantinople. He is then magically transformed into a woman and has numerous adventures through the next three and a quarter centuries, aging only twenty years in the process, to end up as a woman in 1928. No one bats an eyelash in the process, though Orlando does have to go to court to secure her claim to her title and lands—rights she lost when she became a woman.

Orlando's ability to choose her sex is presented as a victory over what Woolf regarded as the arbitrary nature of gender. After the transformation, she writes that "in every other respect, Orlando remained precisely as he had been. The change of sex, though it altered their future, did nothing whatever to alter their identity."

Woolf grew up in the Victorian era, when masculinity and femininity were considered not only fixed but sacrosanct. Even radical thinkers like Sigmund Freud, who famously asserted that "anatomy is destiny," upheld what was considered the natural order of things. As a member of the sexually liberated Bloomsbury set, a group of English writers and artists active in the first part of the twentieth century, Woolf set out to challenge such fallacies. In *Orlando,* she suggests that sex roles are costumes that can be changed at will. Orlando, for example, is not the only fluidly sexed character in the book. The Archduchess Harriet of Finster-Aarhorn and

Scand-op-Boom turns out to be an archduke, and Orlando's sea-captain husband reveals that he has a feminine side, for which she loves him all the more.

Woolf, who was sexually abused by her half-brother as a child, returned to the subject of sex and destiny many times in her writing. In *A Room of One's Own* (1929), for example, she sarcastically refutes the idea that women are incapable of producing work of a comparable quality to men's, by inventing the character of Judith Shakespeare, William's talented sister, who because of her sex is denied the opportunities that turned her brother into the best-loved playwright in history. Within *Orlando*'s whimsical pages, Woolf can give her character a much happier ending. Orlando may be a woman, but she never has to compromise.

TENDER IS THE NIGHT (1934), F. SCOTT FITZGERALD (1896-1940)

Tender Is the Night was Fitzgerald's favorite of his novels. It's also his most nakedly autobiographical, and in the lyricism of its language—the title is a line from Keats—his most poetic. It's also flawed. The characters aren't quite fully realized, the chronology is clunky, and the book's final third reads as a hastily tacked-on ending. Still, as Fitzgerald inscribed in a friend's copy, "*Gatsby* was a tour de force, but this is a confession of faith." *Gatsby* may be what everyone reads in high school, but it's *Tender Is the Night,* his "other" novel, that shows him at the height of his powers, before he burnt out. The book's portrayal of disillusionment could only have come from an author who had lived through it.

It tells the story of Dick and Nicole Diver, a golden couple based in part on Sara and Gerald Murphy, the American expats who acted as literary godparents to the Lost Generation, a group of American writers living abroad in the post–World War I era that included Fitzgerald, Ernest Hemingway, and John Dos Passos. When the novel opens, life seems to be filled with promise for the Divers. They're young and beautiful and in love. Because they're also enormously wealthy, they spend their time traveling around

Europe, enjoying themselves and entertaining their amusing friends, all of whom are enchanted by them.

That's where the comparison to the Murphys, who felt savaged by Fitzgerald's portrayal, ends. The dynamics of the Divers' marriage, the dispiriting aimlessness of their existence, Nicole's fragile mental health—all that is taken from Fitzgerald's own life and relationship with his wife, the Alabama belle Zelda Sayre. It's as though he started out writing about the Murphys and ended up writing about his own troubled marriage. Dick, we learn, was once a promising psychiatrist, and Nicole, who was sexually abused by her father, was his patient. Rather than pursue his career, Dick has elected to live on Nicole's money. Still, all seems to be going well until Nicole has a mental collapse. Though she eventually recovers, Dick begins a downward slide that accelerates after Nicole leaves him for another man. The novel ends with Dick in exile from their idyllic world, moving from one small American backwater to another, while Nicole, now presumably cured, lives happily abroad with her new husband.

Fitzgerald began writing *Tender Is the Night* in 1925, when he and Zelda still were glorying in his success. By the time it was published, in 1934, this early promise had vanished. Zelda had been diagnosed with schizophrenia and spent the rest of her life in and out of psychiatric hospitals. Fitzgerald's popularity had waned, and heavy drinking had taken a toll on his health. He never completed another book. Like Dick Diver, he was far gone from his golden age.

THE PORTABLE DOROTHY PARKER (1944), DOROTHY PARKER (1893–1967)

One of Dorothy Parker's most famous ditties details seven different ways of committing suicide. She had tried several of them, including poison and pills, and found them lacking. And so, she concluded, "You might as well live."

It's this bleak yet resignedly optimistic attitude that shaped Parker's trademark witticisms and that makes them so ruefully funny. She drank heavily, battled depression, unsuccessfully tried to kill herself three times, was divorced twice and married three times (twice to the same man), and was never completely at ease. She also wrote some of the darkest, most wickedly funny poems, short stories, and magazine articles of the twentieth century (when challenged to use the word "horticulture" in a sentence, she shot back, "You can lead a whore to culture, but you can't make her think"), the best of which are collected in *The Portable Dorothy Parker*.

After a stint writing captions at *Vogue*, Parker joined the staff of *Vanity Fair* in 1917, eventually becoming its theater critic. Her reviews were characteristically pithy. "*The House Beautiful* is the play lousy," one began. It was while she was at *Vanity Fair* that Parker, with a few colleagues and friends, including the critic Alexander Woollcott, editor Harold Ross and his journalist wife, Jane Grant, and the playwright and director George S. Kaufman, began having lunch at the Algonquin Hotel on West Forty-fourth Street in Manhattan. These boozy gatherings grew into the Algonquin Round Table, the storied font of Jazz Age wit. In 1925, Ross and Grant cofounded another one of the '20s most cherished relics, *The New Yorker*, a magazine that Parker contributed to for the next thirty years.

She had a killer instinct for the incriminating detail. Of the two self-satisfied office girls walking down Fifth Avenue in "The Standard of Living," she wrote, "[They] set their feet with exquisite precision, as if they stepped over the necks of peasants." But it was Parker's sharply attuned ear for dialogue that gave her writing its particular sting. In "Arrangement in Black and White," written in 1927, she turns the reader into a cringing eavesdropper listening to a bigot prattle on about her lack of bigotry. And she returned again and again to the stilted awkwardness that descends on unhappy couples, a subject she knew intimately.

Parker often disparaged her own writing, dismissing its brevity and lack of gravitas. She tried to write a novel once, thinking it would give her the distinction she thought she lacked, but she found the experience so distressing that she swallowed a bottle of shoe polish. She needn't have. Her succinct and caustic humor is exactly what makes her unique.

THE BELL JAR (1963),
SYLVIA PLATH (1932-1963)

It's the summer of 1953, and Esther Greenwood appears to have it all: She's in New York for a glamorous monthlong stint as one of twelve guest junior editors at a fashion magazine; her tall, handsome, med-school boyfriend is the ideal 1950s American man; and she's poised to start her senior year at one of the Seven Sisters colleges, where she's a straight-A student. But instead of sunning herself in the glow of her perfect life, she's rapidly unraveling. While the other girls enjoy the luncheons and teas the magazine has organized for them, Esther finds herself increasingly disoriented. The ideas of marriage and motherhood terrify her. She's obsessed with the Rosenbergs, a couple found guilty of spying for the Soviets, and their imminent execution. Coming home one night, she looks in the mirror and doesn't recognize herself. When she learns that she's been turned down for a writing class at Harvard and will have to spend the rest of the summer at home in the suburbs, she cracks completely. Madness descends like the bell jar of the title, sealing her off from reality and leaving little room to breathe. After a horrifying bout of electroshock therapy and a botched suicide attempt, she ends up in a psychiatric hospital.

In the four-plus decades since Sylvia Plath's suicide at the age of thirty, her story has assumed epic proportions, partly because of the tragic circumstances of her death—estranged from her husband, the English poet Ted Hughes, she left behind three small children—and partly because of the unrealized promise of the few books of poetry she had published. Reading her mordant, sharply observed words in *The Colossus* or *Ariel,* her brilliance is undeniable; you can't help but wonder where maturity and experience would have taken her. But while Plath is most critically lauded as a poet, it's the autobiographical *The Bell Jar* that has made her a feminist icon.

The book is based on the nervous breakdown and subsequent treatment Plath experienced during her junior year at Smith College, and it's this trapped-on-the-inside view of madness that gives the book its immediacy. Esther's drift into insanity is alarmingly plausible, especially given the expectations placed on women in the early 1950s. But the book is far from a solid wall of depression—it's punctuated with bouts of comic relief that are deliciously black. In the novel's final pages, Esther seems to have come to some sort of truce with the world. While she may never be as perkily conformist as some of her fellow guest editors, neither is she despairing. But the ending's optimism is tinged with wariness, for Plath refuses to be anything less than clear-eyed about Esther's future: "How did I know that someday—at college, in Europe, somewhere, anywhere—the bell jar, with its stifling distortions, wouldn't descend again?"

IN COLD BLOOD (1966), TRUMAN CAPOTE (1924-1984)

Legend has it Truman Capote devised the idea for *In Cold Blood* thanks to a chance reading of a three-hundred-word news item buried in the back pages of the November 15, 1959, edition of *The New York Times*. It described the killing of a Kansas farm family, the Clutters, the previous night. They'd been bound, gagged, and shot in the head at close range. Intrigued, Capote traveled to Kansas, intending to write a magazine article about the murders. He spent the next six years researching the project, which he had quickly decided would make a better book. When *In Cold Blood* was finally published in 1966, Capote claimed to have invented a new literary genre, the nonfiction novel.

The Clutters were a caricature of a 1950s family: clean-cut, close-knit, church- and 4-H-going. Father Herb was a respected town elder, daughter Nancy baked prizewinning cherry pies, and son Kenyon liked to do woodwork. The only incongruous note was Mrs. Clutter, Bonnie, who suffered from depression and had been a semi-invalid for years.

The killers couldn't have been more different from their wholesome victims. Perry Smith's parents were by turns indifferent and abusive, and two of his three siblings committed suicide. He was addicted to aspirin, which he liked to chew, and had delusional daydreams. Richard Hickock was more of a garden-variety hood.

He had a penchant for passing bad checks, liked to run over dogs, and was sexually attracted to young girls. The pair traveled to the Clutter house to steal ten thousand dollars, which they'd been told Herb Clutter kept in a safe in his office. But though the murders put them in the headlines, the underlying robbery was as second-rate as everything else about the pair: Their total haul came to forty dollars, a radio, and a pair of binoculars.

What makes *In Cold Blood* so compelling is Capote's painstaking, if unorthodox, reporting. He interviewed dozens of people for the book, but rather than taking notes, which he considered intrusive, he committed entire conversations to memory, then rushed back to his hotel room to type them up.

The novel made Capote the most famous and celebrated writer in America, though the book wasn't without its detractors, notably the British critic Kenneth Tynan, who felt Capote should have done more to save the accused murderers (they were hanged). It was the pinnacle of Capote's career, as well as the last book he ever finished.

To celebrate the book's publication, Capote gave his famous Black and White Ball, "the party of the century," at New York's Plaza Hotel. Then he started work on a novel called *Answered Prayers,* which he described as an American version of Proust. A few chapters, including the infamous "La Côte Basque," named for the Manhattan restaurant where ladies like Capote's **Swans** lunched, were published in 1975. It turned out to be a salacious, thinly veiled account of the dysfunctional marriage of one of their number, **Babe Paley**. She never forgave him for his betrayal. Ostracized by the social set he'd acted as court jester to, Capote slid into alcoholism and a bloated irrelevance. He died just a few weeks short of his sixtieth birthday.

LOLITA (1955),
VLADIMIR NABOKOV (1899–1977)

"I found myself maturing amid a civilization that allows a man of twenty-five to court a girl of sixteen but not a girl of twelve," mourns Humbert Humbert, the most famous pedophile in literature. This sad-sack European aesthete is nearer forty when he meets the American twelve-year-old of his dreams—though frankly, even a sixteen-year-old would be pushing it—but his predilection for pubescent flesh is stronger than ever, a failing he attributes to an unfulfilled childhood sexual encounter with a charmer named Annabel. Within seconds of spotting Lolita Haze, the long-dead Annabel's doppelgänger, poor old Humbert is hooked.

Lolita is the story of Humbert's sexual obsession with a "nymphet," as he terms the nine- to fourteen-year-old girls he lusts after and whom he must have at any cost. He even marries her mother (who is conveniently dispatched in a freak car accident while Lo's away at summer camp) to be near her. In the end, he loses Lo to another pedophile, whom he then hunts down and kills. The novel takes the form of a confession with which Humbert's lawyer plans to prime the jury at his trial for murder, but it never gets used as such because his client succumbs to a heart attack before legal proceedings begin. Lolita, by now eighteen and married, dies in childbirth not long after. Sudden, cruel death is a frequent occurrence in *Lolita* (Humbert describes his mother's premature demise with a terse, parenthetical "picnic, lightning").

Explicit sex, however, is not. *Lolita* may be notorious for its lubricity—the only publisher Nabokov could initially find to take it on was Olympia Press, the renowned Paris-based purveyor of smut—but its delights are arguably more of the mind than of the body. Nabokov's shimmering prose, a mesmerizing web of wordplay and hilariously inappropriate juxtapositions, caresses the reader into submission—a remarkable feat considering English was not his first language. Factor in the delusional Humbert's unreliability as the novel's sole narrator and you have one deeply ambiguous tale. That's where *Lolita*'s real shock value comes from. Lolita, for all her exasperating brattiness and stupidity, is a child who's essentially her stepfather's sexual slave. And Humbert is pathetic but cunning, as when he waits until after he and Lolita have had sex for the first time to tell her that her mother is dead. That's when he knows he has her: "At the hotel we had separate rooms, but in the middle of the night she came sobbing into mine, and we made it up very gently. You see, she had absolutely nowhere else to go."

Humbert realizes he's a monster, but Nabokov never judges him for it. As he notes in the novel's accompanying essay, *Lolita* "has no moral in tow."

ONE HUNDRED YEARS OF SOLITUDE (1967), GABRIEL GARCÍA MÁRQUEZ (B. 1928)

Nobel Prize winner Gabriel García Márquez's epic *One Hundred Years of Solitude* begins with one of the most intriguing opening sentences in literature: "Many years later, as he faced the firing squad, Colonel Aureliano Buendía was to remember that distant afternoon when his father took him to discover ice." It's typical of the novel's cinematic scope that it takes several pages to arrive at the colonel's memory of the afternoon in question and then several more to realize that the firing squad doesn't kill him. In fact, no one in the book lives or dies in a straightforward manner. In this foremost example of magical realism—a phrase that first described a particular brand of Latin American fiction but has now entered the wider cultural lexicon—past, present, and future coexist, and the supernatural is accepted as fact. Disgruntled ghosts linger in the garden, an insomnia plague grips an entire town, and a woman shrinks to the size of a newborn as she ages. Hauntings and vendettas are the stuff of everyday life.

Though the book zips along at a brisk pace, it would be impossible to summarize the sprawling plot in a paragraph. The narrative follows several generations of the Buendía family, who live in the Edenic hamlet of Macondo in a remote region of an unnamed South American country (though the book is often interpreted as a metaphorical history of García Márquez's native country of Colombia). At the start of the novel, Macondo is "a truly happy village where no one was over thirty years of age and where no one had died," but as civilization encroaches, the Buendías and their fellow Macondans become caught up in both its wonders (ice, telephones) and its uglinesses (colonialism, civil war), and unhappiness, corruption, and violent death enter their lives. As the title suggests, every form of isolation, from literal imprisonment to the joy of being secluded with the one you love, is explored, a paradox that allows García Márquez to swing from tragedy to comedy.

The novel ends when Aureliano II, the last living Buendía, deciphers the prophecies of an old gypsy who had befriended his great-great-great-grandfather José Arcadio Buendía, the town's founding patriarch. As Aureliano II reads them, he realizes that the prophecies are a history of his family from the time they arrived in their jungle home. The text describes the events of his own life, including his reading of the text as he reads it. As he reaches its final lines, an apocalyptic wind comes along and blows him and the now-deserted, vegetation-choked town off the map and out of our human memory. In effect, Aureliano II has destroyed what his ancestor José Arcadio began a hundred years earlier—the Buendías and Macondo are history. He's also doing exactly what we as readers do, closing the book on a world that we've come to know intimately when we arrive at the end of the story.

FIVE ART BOOKS
TO DISPLAY

A BOOKCASE FULL OF literary novels suggests that you've got intellectual depth; a coffee table piled with large-format photo books shows that you've got style, too. An informed eclecticism is the goal here: ironic society portraits, arty photography, and the always reliable allusion to London in the '60s.

A WONDERFUL TIME: AN INTIMATE PORTRAIT OF THE GOOD LIFE, SLIM AARONS (HARPER & ROW, 1974)

Slim Aarons described his photos as "attractive people doing attractive things in attractive places" and that pretty much sums up his mid-seventies classic depicting the rich at play. *A Wonderful Time* took off in the 1990s, when it was adopted by the fashion pack as a touchstone of high-ironic chic, and prices for the out-of-print book soared past a thousand dollars. Photos such as the shot of a group of orange-ily tanned wives—it's impossible to imagine they're anything else—with back-combed hair and baby-doll dresses lounging by the pool in front of one of **Richard Neutra**'s Palm Springs houses inspired **Steven Meisel**'s 2000 Versace ad campaign, though purists may prefer the portrait of **C. Z. Guest**, one of **Truman Capote**'s **Swans**, in white shorts beside yet another pool. Harry N. Abrams published a reissue in 2003, called *Slim Aarons: Once Upon a Time,* but the original carries far more cachet.

THE BALLAD OF SEXUAL DEPENDENCY, NAN GOLDIN (APERTURE, 1986)

Nan Goldin's record of the lives of her "tribe" of friends and acquaintances in the East Village in the 1970s and '80s is a seminal work of photography. Originally presented as a slide show at places like the **Mudd Club**, it's a vivid, astonishingly intimate look at urban bohemia as it was being decimated by drugs and AIDS. Goldin concentrates on the bedrooms, kitchens, and dive bars where small-time dramas get played out, and her forte is documenting the intensity with which these dramas can hurt. In one of the most famous photos in the series, we see her battered face after a beating by her abusive lover, the bruises around her eyes contrasting with her shiny red lipstick. Goldin's raw style and luxurious colors, a result of her use of the flash, have influenced an entire generation of photographers and countless fashion shoots.

THE PHOTOGRAPHS OF RON GALELLA 1960–1990, INTRODUCTION BY TOM FORD (GREYBULL, 2002)

Ron Galella is, if you can imagine such a thing, the grand old man of the paparazzi. He wasn't the first shutterbug to surprise Jackie Onassis as she strolled in Central Park or Marlon Brando as he left a restaurant, but he was certainly the most notorious person ever to combine lurking and photography. Which is why Onassis got a court order to keep him fifty yards away from her and Brando broke his jaw; it's clearly not easy being a professional voyeur. But while Galella's subjects may have been caught unprepared, there's no doubt he made them look great. His black-and-white snaps of Bianca Jagger, Mikhail Baryshnikov, Lee Radziwill, et al., are effortlessly glamorous—so much so that Galella has been resurrected as an icon-making hero by the fashion industry: No less an arbiter than Tom Ford wrote the introduction to this collection of his best shots.

BIRTH OF THE COOL, DAVID BAILEY (VIKING STUDIO, 1999)

Our idea of cool may have developed without the intervention of David Bailey, but it's unlikely that anyone would want to bet on it. As a fashion photographer in the 1960s, the Cockney-born Bailey was a key player in Swinging London. In the process, he became as famous as the rock stars, aristocrats, and actors who posed for him, inspiring the character of the lothario photographer in Michelangelo Antonioni's *Blow-Up*. Along with shots of his girlfriends, models Jean Shrimpton and Penelope Tree, and his then wife, Catherine Deneuve, *Birth of the Cool* includes portraits of Julie Christie, Marianne Faithfull, the Rolling Stones, Mary Quant, and East End gangsters the Kray twins. In short, it's a visual history of a period that continues to inspire fashion, film, and photography by someone who was there when it happened.

DIANE ARBUS: REVELATIONS (RANDOM HOUSE, 2003)

From the 1950s until her suicide at the age of forty-eight in 1971, Diane Arbus (who was one of **Alexey Brodovitch**'s students) photographed people on the fringes of society: nudists, transvestites, circus performers, the mentally disabled. Once seen, her images are unforgettable. From the staring twin girls to the giant towering over his parents, she photographed her subjects with such intimacy that there's no room to look away. You have no choice but to absorb the tenderness of her gaze. To her critics, however, she was a morbid voyeur. **Susan Sontag** wrote that to Arbus, the U.S. was "just a freak show, a wasteland." But to Arbus, freaks were nature's elite. "Most people go through life dreading they'll have a traumatic experience," she wrote. "Freaks are born with their trauma. They're aristocrats."

TEN WORKS OF ART
TO BE FAMILIAR WITH

TALKING ABOUT ART scares people, and with good reason—critics and academics have built up such a wall of obtuse jargon and self-referential observations around it that it's easy to feel like you need a Ph.D. to venture an opinion. In fact, you just need a bit of background in art history.

LE DÉJEUNER SUR L'HERBE (1863), EDOUARD MANET (1832-1883)

In 1863, the year *Le Déjeuner sur l'herbe (Luncheon on the Grass)* was painted, art was at a stalemate. In France, the only art that was exhibited was in the heavy, academic style sanctioned by the French Academy, which determined what subjects were worthy of portrayal, what techniques were valid, what was beau-

> **PRONUNCIATION GUIDE**
>
> **Edouard Manet, *Le Déjeuner sur l'herbe*:**
> **eh-doo-AHR ma-NEH,**
> **luh day-jzhuh-NAY SUR LAIRB**

tiful. The Academy's tastemaking power was most evident in its annual Salon, to which only artists who stuck to the official program of mythological scenes and classically inspired portraits—i.e., the sort of art that coordinates with the curtains—were invited to exhibit. When the Academy's selection committee rejected *Le Déjeuner sur l'herbe,* Manet decided he'd had enough. He and some like-minded colleagues got together and organized the Salon des Réfusés, or Show of the Refused. It was at this pointedly confrontational exhibit that *Le Déjeuner* was first seen.

The painting depicts two couples having a picnic in a sun-dappled wood. Though the poses are taken from the old masters, the couples are clearly members of the contemporary bourgeoisie. The men are rather jauntily dressed, while the women are just as jauntily not dressed—one has stripped to the flesh and gazes coolly out at the viewer; the other crouches in the background in a loose interpretation of ancient attire. It's an awkward, unsettling painting; the landscape looks oddly artificial, and the strangeness of the situation is left unexplained. Certainly the subject matter was considered dangerously weird and lewd at the time, but it was Manet's handling of the paint that really disgusted critics. His blocky colors and flat swaths of paint were sharply, spikily new. For the members of the Academy and their ilk, this was not only unseemly but morally questionable.

Not everyone, however, was so bound to the past. The poet and critic Baudelaire considered Manet to be in the vanguard of contemporary art, a style that eventually came to be known as **impressionism**. This movement didn't really get under way for another three years or so, when Claude Monet painted *Terrace à Ste. Adresse,* but its tenets—natural light, outdoor settings, fragmented colors, modern subjects—are all present in embryo form in *Le Déjeuner.* Today, its relentless sunniness makes impressionism one of the most popular and accessible styles of painting in the world. In the 1860s, however, it was cutting-edge stuff. Impressionism changed the way people looked at art. They no longer expected subjects to pose like Greek gods or be flanked by swags of implausible drapery. And in their loose handling of paint, the impressionists foreshadowed abstraction, one of the dominant themes of twentieth-century art.

LES DEMOISELLES D'AVIGNON (1907),
PABLO PICASSO (1881–1973)

No matter how daring painters had been in the four-hundred-odd years that stretched between the Renaissance and the turn of the twentieth century, there was one constraint they couldn't seem to break free of: one-point perspective. Even the most radical among them—**Manet**, Paul Cézanne—continued to paint canvases that strove to appear three-dimensional, with objects receding to the vanishing point. So when Picasso unveiled *Les Demoiselles d'Avignon*, with its flattened forms and fractured treatment of space, to a group of friends in 1907, they knew immediately that he'd achieved something monumental. The painting was almost ominous in its ability to shock, a power that it retains today, a century after it was painted. In fact, some among that first group of viewers found its antagonism overwhelming, and urged Picasso to scrap it. Though he didn't go that far, he didn't exactly promote *Les Demoiselles* either: It wasn't publicly exhibited until 1916. You get the impression that Picasso was a little afraid of what he had created.

> **PRONUNCIATION GUIDE**
>
> *Les Demoiselles d'Avignon:*
> **LAY de-mwah-ZEL**
> **DAV-ee-nyoh**

The painting portrays a group of five prostitutes in a brothel (it was named for a well-known one in Barcelona). Their stances are confrontational, their stares belligerent. One appears to be squatting over a bidet. Disturbingly, Picasso has chosen to paint them as fragmented, garishly hued planes with hatchetlike faces that recall early Iberian sculpture and African masks. He's completely disregarded the idea of traditional perspective. Everything, even the air around the women, appears to be shattered.

Les Demoiselles d'Avignon is not a beautiful painting. In fact, it's downright ugly and has been interpreted as both evidence of the artist's misogyny and an indictment of colonialism. But there's no denying its aggressive, primal vitality—or its importance. It's not an exaggeration to say that *Les Demoiselles* shook the art world to its core. Within a few years of its completion, **cubism**, which took three-dimensional forms and broke them into flat areas of color, had become the prevailing mode in art, and the standard by which every progressive painter was measured. Artists embraced the new style, but the public eye took a while to adjust. At the Armory Show in New York in 1913, the first major exhibit of cubist art, seminal works such as **Marcel Duchamp**'s *Nude Descending a Staircase* (1912) were lampooned. But the die was cast. After *Les Demoiselles,* nothing in art was the same.

FOUNTAIN (1917),
MARCEL DUCHAMP (1887–1968)

By 1913, Marcel Duchamp had become bored with what he termed "retinal" art, or art that was purely visual. He'd been painting in the cubist style, but this had rapidly moved from the artistic vanguard to its new standard. Eager to test the open-mindedness of the art world, Duchamp conceived of the readymade, ordinary manufactured objects that he chose, titled, and signed. In doing so, he implied, he elevated them to the status of art. The new status of these objects wasn't always apparent to others, however: One of his early readymades, a cast-iron bottle rack, was accidentally discarded by his sister in a fit of overzealous housekeeping.

More successful was *Fountain,* a porcelain urinal that Duchamp signed *R. Mutt* and submitted to the Society of Independent Artists in New York, of which he was a director. The Society rejected *Fountain,* but when it was discovered that R. Mutt was really Duchamp, the work was accepted. Disgusted, Duchamp promptly resigned from the society.

His attitude was typical of the **dada** movement, which had started as an international protest against the First World War. Dadaists were punks: They wanted to destroy values they viewed as hypocritical and outdated and replace them with anarchic, irrational ones (even the name "dada" is nonsensical). At performance spaces such as the Cabaret Voltaire in Zurich, one of the main centers of dada, a typical evening might consist of Tristan Tzara tearing up pieces of paper and letting them fall randomly to make "chance" collages, while Hugo Ball recited nonsense poetry that consisted of nonverbal sounds. In 1919, Duchamp painted a mustache and goatee on a print of da Vinci's *Mona Lisa* and called it *L.H.O.O.Q.,* which when read out loud letter by letter in French sounds like *Elle a chaud au cul* (she's got a hot ass). Puerile, yes, but typical of the level of dada discourse.

Though *Fountain* is an important work of art in its own right, it's the provocative posturing that Duchamp and his cohorts adopted that proved to be incredibly influential to subsequent generations of artists and makes him one of the most important artists of the twentieth century. Duchamp's spiritual children include such innovators as Robert Rauschenberg and Jasper Johns, whose merging of painting and mass-produced images and objects taken from everyday life—magazine photos, beer cans, flags—presaged **pop art**, and the Fluxus artists, who experimented with blending various artistic media and disciplines to create "happenings." At one such event, called *Cut Piece* (1964), Fluxus artist Yoko Ono invited audience members to cut away pieces of her clothing in a performance that was intended as a comment on gender inequality. By proposing that art is an idea, not a narrowly defined creation, and that it could be made from anything, Duchamp and the dadaists set the course for much of modern art.

OBJECT (LUNCHEON IN FUR) (1936), MERET OPPENHEIM (1913–1985)

In 1924, an ex–medical orderly named André Breton published a paper called *Manifesto of Surrealism.* The densely worded, forty-page-long essay called for a new form of art and literature, one that would tap into the subliminal mind and in doing so free people from the conventions that bound them. "Our unceasing wish, growing more and more urgent from day to day," he proclaimed, "has been at all costs to avoid considering a system of thought as a refuge." In his *Second Manifesto of Surrealism*—for a group bent on complete creative emancipation, the **surrealists** were remarkably specific—Breton elaborated on his theme: "The simplest Surrealist act consists of dashing down into the street, pistol in hand, and firing blindly, as fast as you can pull the trigger, into the crowd." To the surrealists, who included former **dada**ists such as Breton and Man Ray, as well as Salvador Dalí, Jean Cocteau (a favorite collaborator of couturier

Elsa Schiaparelli's), and René Magritte, the rational mind was an obstacle to creative expression, a barrier to be pulled down. Taking their cue from Sigmund Freud's fashionable new theories about the unconscious, they saw repressed memories and dreams as catalysts. But where Freud saw the exploring of the unconscious as therapy, the surrealists saw the unconscious as an artistic playground waiting to be mapped. Dreams, with their odd juxtapositions and myriad symbols of sex and violence—there is a strong misogynistic streak in surrealism—were a special interest of theirs.

It's against this backdrop that *Luncheon in Fur,* a fur-covered tea-cup, saucer, and spoon, was created. An audacious and original artist, the Berlin-born Oppenheim was the only widely recognized female member of the movement. She was also a feminist whose work made frequent allusions to female sexuality and the oppression of women by a patriarchal society, a stance that couldn't have been easy to maintain in that particular group. *Luncheon in Fur* takes an everyday object and makes it strange, even ridiculous. It also suggests the unpleasant sensation of actually drinking from such a cup. And finally, it recalls female genitalia. The mix of humor, provocation, and sex make it a surrealist icon.

Shortly after its creation, Oppenheim went into a creative crisis and didn't make any art for years. It wasn't until the late 1950s that she became active again, and in the late 1960s, when the work of female artists began to receive serious attention, she was rediscovered by critics. But while her output was limited, with *Luncheon in Fur,* Oppenheim created a remarkable piece. She took something ordinary and made it extraordinary. Compared with the elaborately executed paintings of better-known surrealists such as Dalí or Magritte, her eloquent simplicity is even more memorable.

NUMBER 1, 1950 (LAVENDER MIST) (1950), JACKSON POLLOCK (1912-1956)

Jackson Pollock towers over American art. Hard-drinking and prolific, he was the first American artist to achieve celebrity status. He was on the cover of *Life,* a magazine read by people in suburbs and small towns, not aesthetes who went to gallery openings. He was filmed and photographed making his paintings, which were as huge and sprawling and restless as the West he grew up in. And by dying in a car crash while still fairly young, he achieved the ultimate American hero's end, the kind that can push a man to icon status. Nine days after his death, *Time* magazine eulogized him as "the bearded shock trooper of modern painting."

Pollock originally studied with the American regionalist Thomas Hart Benton, and his early work is figurative. It wasn't until the late 1940s that he laid his canvases flat on the floor and began experimenting with his drip technique, in which he built up layer upon layer of thick, weblike color, a method inspired by Navajo sand painting. Though this splattering sounds anarchic, Jack the Dripper was a graceful and methodical painter. Footage of him at work shows him so absorbed in his balletic reverie that he could dance around an oblong of canvas for half an hour without stopping to rest.

His dexterity is immediately evident when you look at *Lavender Mist,* his most intense and powerful work. Though enormous—it's more than six and a half feet tall and almost thirteen feet wide—it is also, as its name suggests, astonishingly delicate. Pollock's control of the paint is apparent in the clarity of his colors: the whorls of dusty pink, the scratches of white, the lacy swirls of black. As a whole, they convey raw, crackling energy; separately, they're as ethereal and refined as anything painted by the **impressionists**. It's a bewitching painting—you can't stand before *Lavender Mist* and not feel entangled in its sinewy emotions. Like a force of nature, it completely dominates the room that it hangs in at the National Gallery of Art in Washington, D.C.

Though Pollock only painted in this style for four years, it's become synonymous with his career and with the upswing of **abstract expressionism**, the movement that in the 1940s and 1950s was instrumental in shifting the focus of the art world from Paris to New York. As a group, the abstract expressionists, who included Pollock; his wife, Lee Krasner; Mark Rothko; and Willem de Kooning, believed that the most valid subject for art was inner conflict; they had a romantic view of the artist as an alienated loner, creating art that confronted the hypocrisies of contemporary life. More than sixty years after abstract expressionism was born, it's a view that continues to have currency, a phenomenon whose trail can be traced directly to Pollock's paint-splattered studio.

A BIGGER SPLASH (1967),
DAVID HOCKNEY (B. 1937)

Just as it took a transplant to southern California, **Richard Neutra**, to build the ultimate L.A. house, it took one to create the ultimate L.A. painting: David Hockney, a leading **pop art** star and a Brit who went to Los Angeles on holiday in the early '60s and didn't leave. Instead, he started painting pictures of swimming pools, a backyard phenomenon that fascinated him after the dreariness of postwar Britain.

Hockney was initially drawn to L.A. by John Rechy's homo-erotic novel *City of Night* (1963), about a male hustler, and a lot of the pool paintings feature pretty boys sunbathing naked or emerging wet and dripping from the water. Like his fellow artist/celebrity/social gadfly **Andy Warhol**, whom he later befriended, the bleach-blond Hockney offered a fey rebuke to the macho posturing of the art world—even when he's dealing with controversial subjects, he's chipper and domestic, and his palette is pastel. One of his most famous paintings is *Mr. and Mrs. Clark and Percy* (1971), a portrait of fashion designer **Ossie Clark**, a friend from his student days, and his wife, Celia Birtwell. They're in their living room, posed as though they were sitting for Gainsborough but dressed for 1970s Notting Hill. That Clark was gay and the marriage strained is buried beneath Hockney's guileless brushstrokes.

Hockney's pool series reached its apex in the cheery emptiness of *A Bigger Splash,* which captures the second that follows a diver's entry into the water. The diver who's left behind *A Bigger Splash* has, for the moment, slipped beneath the surface, so that all we see is what's on the surface: a diving board that juts from the lower right toward the center of the canvas, an expanse of blue pool succeeded by the browns and creams of a large-windowed bungalow, and a cloudless sky punctuated by two tall palm trees. The only tension breaking the smooth, flat horizontals and verticals of the painting are the white squiggles and striations of the splash, which rear up like a lacy fountain. It's ostensibly a feel-good painting, but stirring beneath the stillness is a faint sense of unease about the good life that more puritanical or cerebral types—take your pick—often feel about Southern California. As in John Cheever's 1964 short story "The Swimmer" (which is set in the affluent suburbs of New York City), the pool represents despair as well as material success. Hockney may have found paradise in L.A., but his English soul evidently wasn't entirely comfortable with it.

THE DINNER PARTY (1974–1979), JUDY CHICAGO (B. 1939)

Despite the best efforts of the Guerrilla Girls, a group of under-cover feminist artists who once conducted a "weenie count" at New York's Metropolitan Museum of Art (their not-so-shocking con-clusion: only 5 percent of the artists in the Met's modern art collec-tion were female), you don't hear very much about art and feminism anymore. But that may change now that the Brooklyn Museum has opened a new center for feminist art, which includes a triangu-lar room specifically designed for the permanent exhibition of Judy Chicago's monumental installation *The Dinner Party,* which is un-doubtedly the most provocative feminist artwork ever made.

The Dinner Party's mission is a bold one: It seeks to redress the way history has marginalized or ignored women, by giving them their metaphorical place at the table. The piece consists of a three-sided table with seats for 39 guests, all of them mythical or actual female figures. They range from heroines of the ancient world (the Greek poet Sappho, the British warrior queen Boudicca), through to historical figures (Eleanor of Aquitaine, Elizabeth I of England) and twentieth-century artists (**Virginia Woolf**, Georgia O'Keeffe). The names of a further 999 women are inscribed in tiles on the floor. Each place setting includes an embroidered runner that in-corporates symbols from that woman's life and a ceramic plate dec-orated with vividly colored, individualized, fairly explicit sculptures that represent her genitals.

That's where Chicago ran into problems. Though we see phallic shapes all the time and think nothing of them, most of us shrink in horror from too-graphic feminine iconography, convinced it's not nice. Though five thousand people came to the opening in San Fran-cisco, and many of them said it was a life-changing experience, *The Dinner Party* was dismissed by major critics like Robert Hughes ("mainly cliché . . . with colors worthy of a Taiwanese souvenir factory") and Hilton Kramer. Their disdain brings to mind the famous remark Mandy Rice-Davies made at the height of the Profumo Affair, when she was told that one of the politicians involved had denied having an affair with her: "Well, he would, wouldn't he?"

By using traditionally feminine crafts such as embroidery and china painting, Chicago and the small army of volunteers who worked on *The Dinner Party* reclaimed them as valid art forms, a consequence that's benefited countless artists. They were certainly an optimistic, **Germaine Greer**–reading crew; in the film *Right Out of History: The Making of Judy Chicago's "Dinner Party,"* one of them says, "We are not only documenting feminist history, we are in the process of building a feminist approach to the world." They'd probably be surprised to know that it's taken this long for *The Dinner Party* to find a home.

UNTITLED FILM STILLS (1977-1980), CINDY SHERMAN (B. 1954)

Shot between 1977 and 1980, Cindy Sherman's *Untitled Film Stills* are based on the movie publicity stills of the 1950s and '60s. But rather than using models or actresses as her subjects, Sherman's put herself in every frame. The black-and-white photos, sixty-nine in total, feature the artist in costume as a series of instantly recognizable cinematic types: the busty librarian (#13), the young secretary in the big city (#21), the chorus girl with a heart of gold (#15), the smoldering **Italian neorealist** housewife (#35), etc. That we can instantly identify them is the key to this series' success, a condition Sherman was counting on: She ended the series when she ran out of clichés.

Sherman's alone in each shot, but her very deliberate poses suggest that there's someone off camera, watching her. It's unclear what's going on, and the generally blank expressions she wears hint rather than reveal. It's left to the viewer to construct the narrative that these images illustrate.

The photos were taken mostly in Sherman's apartment and at various locations around New York, but she's deliberately made the settings so ambiguous that they could have been taken anywhere. In the same vein, Sherman shows herself to be a very competent chameleon, looking completely different in each guise. Using wigs,

In her proper suit and hat, Cindy Sherman looks like one of the legions of career girls who appeared in 1950s films like The Best of Everything *(1959).*

makeup, and a collection of vintage clothes, she's taken what women do every day—construct an image—and pushed it to extremes.

What makes *Untitled Film Stills* a landmark of **postmodern** art is its appropriation of mass-media techniques to comment on contemporary society. The photos aren't re-creations; Sherman wasn't trying to make exact replicas of the original stills. Each has an element of artifice—an exposed camera cord, a slightly off-kilter angle—that takes it out of the realm of the ordinary and of the original. All the elements of the archetype are there, but the meaning and the intent have been changed. Moreover, the photos are self-consciously self-referential. Unlike previous artists who'd mined pop culture for their work, Sherman didn't approach it as a subject matter or a source of inspiration. Instead, she lifted an entire visual vocabulary from the vernacular of the film still, and then used it to say things that the originals never did. Though various photos from the series were exhibited over the years, it wasn't until 1997 that the entire collection was shown together, at the Museum of Modern Art in New York. In a fitting twist, the show was sponsored by Madonna.

CHARLES THE FIRST (1982), JEAN-MICHEL BASQUIAT (1960–1988)

The Wall Street–driven art boom of the 1980s created many stars—Julian Schnabel, Keith Haring, Eric Fischl, Mark Kostabi— but few have the cultural resonance of Jean-Michel Basquiat. Though critical opinion on him remains divided, his angry, confrontational work and archetypically tragic trajectory, mythologized in numerous articles and in Schnabel's 1996 biopic, *Basquiat,* have ensured him folk-hero status.

The half-Haitian, half–Puerto Rican, Brooklyn-born Basquiat had a comfortable middle-class upbringing, but he didn't have any formal art training. Like his friend Haring, he first came to the attention of the art world via graffiti—in the late 1970s, he and a friend covered lower Manhattan in cryptic communiqués signed *SAMO,* shorthand for "same old shit." His first formal show came in 1980, when he participated in a group exhibit called The Times Square Show, where he caught the attention of the poet/art critic/ Factory habitué René Ricard. Ricard subsequently wrote a hagiographic profile of the young artist called "The Radiant Child" for *Artforum.* The piece launched Basquiat's career—by 1982, he was an art-world darling. His mercurial rise so perfectly embodied the overheated state of the art market that *The New York Times Magazine* made him its cover boy for a 1985 story called "New Art, New Money: The Marketing of an American Artist." Basquiat was living proof of his friend and collaborator **Andy Warhol**'s prediction that art would one day be packaged and promoted like anything else.

Basquiat's output was vast in relation to his fleeting career. He could churn out a painting in a few hours, and one of the gallerists who represented him reportedly kept him semihostage in her basement, sliding drugs and takeout food under the door whenever the production line slowed. Inevitably, this led to a lot of inferior work, which, coupled with the fact that his real importance is arguably what he symbolized rather than what he produced, makes it hard to choose a good representative Basquiat painting. *Charles the First,* though sketchy, contains many of his preferred themes. A black artist in a white art world, Basquiat made frequent allusions to race in his work, with references to black athletes and musicians especially prominent. *Charles the First* is a tribute to the jazz giant Charlie Parker, his preeminent idol (and his fellow drug casualty). The three panels of the painting, blocked off in oblongs of yellow, blue, and black, are covered in Basquiat's trademark scrawl. Along with the name of one of Parker's recordings, "Cherokee," and a reference to his daughter, the painting includes Basquiat's signature crown symbol. At the bottom, he's written his poignant epitaph for Parker: All Young Kings Get Thier [*sic*] Heads Cut Off.

In hindsight, Basquiat's early demise seems inevitable, writes his biographer, Phoebe Hogan: "Take someone with the emotional maturity of a child who aspires to be the Charlie Parker of painting. Place him in a pressure-cooker art world where quantity matters more than quality, aggressive art dealers push prices through the roof, avaricious new collectors speculate wildly, auction houses create instant inflation, and the media magnifies the entire circus through a hyperbolic lens. Add the race card, drugs, and promiscuity at every level. Then call it the burnout of an art star."

LEIGH BOWERY (SEATED) (1990), LUCIAN FREUD (B. 1922)

"I found him perfectly beautiful," said Lucian Freud of Leigh Bowery. It's not a lighthearted remark. Bowery, the Australian-born performance artist who achieved cultural renown in 1980s London for his extravagant, fetish-inspired costumes—a typical Monday-morning outfit might include a latex bodysuit topped with a pig's mask and a bobby's helmet; he saved his more outrageous flights of fancy for when he performed with his S&M-inspired band, Minty—was a mountain of a man with a uniquely lumpy physiognomy. But Freud, who's often referred to as the greatest living realist painter, is no run-of-the-mill portraitist. He's a grand-

MAJOR ART MOVEMENTS AND HOW THEY FIT TOGETHER

Before it became the art of choice for dentists' waiting rooms, the loose brushstrokes of **impressionism** (1874–early twentieth century) were a snub to the stifling academic painting of the mid-nineteenth century. • The emphasis of **art nouveau** (1880s–c. 1919) was on the boldly rendered line, whether that was curved or geometric. • **Fauvism** (1905–c. 1908) was named for the wild beasts to which critics compared its strong colors and rough brushwork. • **Cubism** (1907–1930s) broke the hold that one-point perspective had on art, paving the way for abstraction. • The readymades and *épater le bourgeois* attitude of dada (c. 1916–1920s) brought a sense of the absurd to art. • **Surrealism** (c. 1920–present) picked up where dada left off, by delving deeper into the unconscious and dream imagery. • The streamlined style of **art deco** (early 1920s–c. 1939) was the prevailing design aesthetic of the period between the wars. • **Abstract expressionism** (1940s–1950s) was an American movement that combined emotional intensity and an antifigurative aesthetic. • **Pop art** (1950s–1960s) drew on ideas and techniques found in popular culture, like comic books and silk screening, with deliberately kitsch results. • The stripped-down, geometric experiments of **minimalism** (1960s–1980s) were a reaction to the more painterly style of abstract expressionism. • **Conceptual art** (1960s–present) holds as its premise that the concept behind a work of art is its most important component. • **Postmodernism** (late twentieth century–present) is notoriously tricky to define. Rather than a well-demarcated movement, it's a catchall phrase that describes a lot of art, particularly that which exhibits those quintessentially modern qualities, irony and self-awareness.

son of the founder of psychoanalysis, Sigmund Freud, and if too much has been made of the family bond by some reviewers, it's nevertheless a provocative connection, especially in this case. Lucian Freud's been accused of savagery toward his subjects, but in Bowery, he found one who could meet his merciless gaze head on.

Leigh Bowery (Seated) was the first in a series of portraits Freud painted of Bowery, who though dying of AIDS at the time, posed for him almost daily for two years. Bowery is naked, as Freud's subjects frequently are. It's a condition he renders unsparingly: Nipples sprawl, scrotums sag like fleshy mushrooms, and varicose veins mottle the flesh. Even Kate Moss, who posed for Freud while pregnant, looks distinctly worse for the wear. That Bowery, who was habitually covered from the tip of his bald head to his platform-booted soles, is here stripped of his disguises (he even shaved his body hair for the sitting) makes him even more of an arresting figure—this is his ultimate performance. He's like some ancient colossus, facing us impassively from his throne (actually a red armchair). His belly sags and his left leg and arm are draped over the arm of the chair, giving us a view of the insides of his thighs, which are covered with ominous cuts and dark patches. His translucent skin—Freud commented on it, saying it was like "seeing under the carpet"—is colored in shades that range from violet to gray, as though Freud had examined Bowery inch by inch and was determined to convey what he saw in extreme detail. The murkiness of the palette suggests mud or some equally primeval substance. It's a portrait that's both human and monumental, rather like Bowery himself. Looking at it, it's evident why Freud has been compared to such skillful humanists as Rembrandt and Velázquez. But while the old masters delighted in beauty, Freud's sensuality is more like that of **Diane Arbus**'s—he's attuned to the grotesque. It's no coincidence that he wears a butcher's apron when he paints.

FIVE ARTISTS
TO WATCH

THOUGH ART STARS COME and, more frequently, go, these five have all transcended their initial modishness. Their work is sought after by serious collectors, displayed in museums, and discussed over dinner tables. In other words, don't look blank when their names come up.

JOHN CURRIN (B. 1962)

Are John Currin's buxom babes evidence of an arrested sexuality or subversive social commentary? Whichever way you interpret them, it's hard not to stare. As the critic Peter Schjeldahl wrote of Currin's work in *The New Yorker*, "He demonstrates the power of the aesthetic to overrule our normal taste, morality and intellectual convictions." What makes loopily **surrealist** paintings like *Stanford After-Brunch* (2000), which depicts a gaggle of WASPy, post–Carrie Bradshaw suburban matrons, so irresistible is their technical prowess. Currin's sensibility may suggest *Playboy*—and sometimes Norman Rockwell gets thrown into the mix—but his elongated, distorted figures owe a debt to Lucas Cranach. In any case, Currin is almost certainly the only artist ever to have appeared in both the Whitney Museum of American Art, which gave him a midcareer retrospective, and *Juggs,* the porn mag dedicated to dirigible-size breasts. His paintings of his wife, fellow artist Rachel Feinstein, were the inspiration for Marc Jacobs's autumn 2004 collection.

LISA YUSKAVAGE (B. 1962)

Like **John Currin**, to whom her work is often compared, Lisa Yuskavage paints cartoonishly pneumatic women. But while Currin's inspiration is the Northern Renaissance, Yuskavage's kitschy style has its roots in the kind of junk-shop paintings that depict topless women strumming guitars. Hers is an exclusively feminine dream-world, in which amply endowed models seem mesmerized by their own voluptuousness. The button-nosed blonde in *Day* (2000), for example, lifts her top to study her breasts like she's just noticed they're there. Even Yuskavage's painting style is luscious—light drips across her canvases like melted honey. But under all the camp she's a transgressive artist, prodding at stereotypes and challenging the male gaze even as she panders to it. She gives her nudes an inner life that suggests that all is not well in the Playboy Mansion, and in doing so raises issues of female desire and sexuality that make a lot of people squirm.

> **PRONUNCIATION GUIDE**
>
> **Lisa Yuskavage:**
> **LEE-sa**
> **you-SKAHV-edge**

TRACEY EMIN (B. 1963)

Along with her fellow Young British Artist (YBA) Damien Hirst, Tracey Emin is no stranger to controversy. Her work is sexual, confessional, and often alarmingly frank. But then, as she is the first to admit, sex has been a consistent and often distressing theme in her life. She was raped when she was thirteen, and her memoir, *Strangeland* (2006), details further sexual abuse. One of her first brushes with notoriety came in 1995, with an installation called *Everyone I Have Ever Slept With 1963–1995,* a tent she embroidered with the names of everyone she'd ever shared a bed with, including family members she'd slept with as a child and her two aborted fetuses (the installation was subsequently destroyed in a fire). She followed this up with another installation, the Turner Prize–nominated *My Bed* (1999), which features her unmade bed, complete with stained sheets, used condoms, and bloody underwear. Her provocative subject matter didn't prevent the French luxury label Longchamps from hiring her to design a luggage line decorated with her trademark embroidery in 2005.

MATTHEW BARNEY (B. 1967)

The media artist and filmmaker Matthew Barney, who's been deemed "the most important American artist of his generation," is best known for his densely symbolic, vividly imagined *Cremaster Cycle* of films. Eight years in the making, the five-part series (which was not made in order) is part autobiography, part national myth, part meditation on creativity. The series has almost no dialogue and a byzantine symbolic structure, but it's surprisingly easy to watch. Subjects caught up in *Cremaster*'s epic sweep include Mormonism, Masonic rites, Celtic legends, the architecture of **Frank Lloyd Wright**, satyrs and nymphs, and Harry Houdini, who's played by Norman Mailer. And then there's the cremaster itself, which is the muscle that connects the scrotum to the body. According to Barney, there are complicated esoteric connections among all these seemingly unconnected phenomena. A more recent film, *Drawing Restraint 9,* was made in collaboration with his longtime girlfriend, Björk.

KARA WALKER (B. 1969)

In her room-size tableaux, Kara Walker takes a genteel eighteenth-century parlor craft, the paper silhouette, in which a subject's profile is cut out of paper and mounted against a contrasting color, and appropriates it to depict the dynamics of race and sexuality in America. Her catalyst is African American history, particularly slavery and its legacy. Walker doesn't shy away from provocation: works like *Atlanta: Being the Narrative of a Negress in the Flames of Desire—A Reconstruction* show extreme sexual violence, a depiction that's made all the more unsettling by the fact that the figures are life-size. Reaction to her work tends to break along generation lines, with many older African American artists accusing Walker, who's also African American, of perpetuating negative stereotypes. Writing about Walker in *The Village Voice,* the critic Jerry Saltz remarked, "Older blacks feel that images of mammies, pickaninnies, and Sambos are irredeemably evil. . . . Younger people assume all images are unstable projections, subject to change. As always, both camps ignore how good art can lift you above the problem and change lives."

TEN CDs TO HAVE IN YOUR COLLECTION

WHEN YOU'RE A TEENAGER, music defines your entire life, from the way you dress to the people you associate with. Though that musical omnipotence fades with age, it never really disappears—hence the discreet perusal of the CD racks of new acquaintances and prospective mates. With these in your collection, you have nothing to worry about.

KIND OF BLUE (1959), MILES DAVIS (1926–1991)

Over the span of a career that lasted nearly forty years, Miles Davis reinvented himself constantly. As a result, there's a record in his considerable output for every type of jazz fan. From the pure bebop of *Steamin' With the Miles Davis Quintet* (1956) to the **hip-hop**-foreshadowing funk-fusion of *On the Corner* (1972), he didn't disappoint. But the Miles album that appeals to everyone, even people who think they don't like jazz, is undoubtedly *Kind of Blue*.

The album is legendary enough to warrant its own biography (*Kind of Blue: The Making of the Miles Davis Masterpiece*, by Ashley

Kahn), but don't let the advance hype turn you off. Music writers love to toss around words like "classic" and "definitive," but in this case, the praise isn't overstated, it's dead-on: *Kind of Blue* is sublime. Though its sound is spare and hushed, the album's overriding characteristic is its voluptuousness—which may be why it's been called the ultimate seduction music (Kahn quotes an authority on this: Anthony Kiedis of the Red Hot Chili Peppers). From the first languorous bass lines and feather-light percussive strokes of "So What," you're lulled into a sort of heavy-eyed trance, one that's sustained through the easygoing keyboard virtuosity of "Freddie Freeloader" and the plaintive trumpet on "Blue in Green." Coming to the end of the final track, the Latin-tinged "Flamenco Sketches," is like emerging blinking into the light after a night with your true love.

What makes *Kind of Blue* all the more astonishing is that it was recorded in just nine hours, and only one of the tracks ("Flamenco Sketches") needed more than one take. All the others were perfect on the first try. In a sense, it's the ultimate tribute to the kind of free-flowing, improvisational jazz Davis was playing at the time, which went on to be hugely influential. The music, as Bill Evans noted in the liner notes, wasn't scored—Davis sketched outlines of the tunes just hours before they were recorded. The rest was up to the all-star band: Evans on piano (except for "Freddie Freeloader," for which Wynton Kelly stepped in), John Coltrane and Julian "Cannonball" Adderley on saxophones, Paul Chambers on bass, and Jimmy Cobb on drums. The tracks they laid down over two days in 1959 went on to become jazz standards, but it was their talent that made them the, yes, classics they are. As Cobb later said, "We just went ahead and did it."

LADY IN SATIN (1958), BILLIE HOLIDAY (1915–1959)

By 1958, Billie Holiday's once supple voice was nothing but a memory. The sultry softness she brought to songs like "Lover Man" and "Strange Fruit" in the 1930s, when she wore white gardenias in her hair and was known as Lady Day, was gone. In its place was the scarred, weakened rasp of a junkie in the grip of a crippling heroin habit. Holiday was only forty-three when she made *Lady in Satin,* but she sounds thirty years older, and her range is just a fraction of what she'd once had. Yet the album, one of the singer's favorites of her own recordings, is mesmerizing.

What makes it such a compelling—and harrowing—listening experience is the bittersweet knowledge that Holiday was once such a promising talent. She was discovered singing in a Harlem nightclub in 1933 by John Hammond, who arranged for her to record with bands like Benny Goodman's. Within a few years, she was a star. But by the early 1940s, she had started using hard drugs, and her career began its inevitable free fall, a descent that was exacerbated by her genius for getting involved with the wrong men, notably her manager, Joe Glaser. In 1947 he set her up on a drug-possession charge with the FBI, allegedly so they'd turn a blind eye to the marijuana use of his more lucrative client Louis Armstrong. Holiday's conviction meant that she was no longer eligible for the work permit necessary to sing in New York clubs where alcohol was served, a factor that effectively curtailed her career.

By the time she walked into the studio to record *Lady in Satin,* she knew she'd lost everything she once had, and this comes through in the raw, blues intensity she brings to otherwise vanilla standards like "You Don't Know What Love Is" and "Glad to Be Unhappy." The album may feature silky string arrangements and an image of the evening gown–clad singer on the cover, but easy listening this is not: When Holiday stretches her ravaged voice on "I'm a Fool to Want You," she projects the accumulated pain and longing of a woman who's seen it all and knows how it ends— badly. It's a desperate and brave recording, and a fitting cap to Holiday's career. A year and half after *Lady in Satin* was released, she died of cirrhosis of the liver in a New York City hospital, with just $750 to her name.

THE SONGS OF LEONARD COHEN (1968), LEONARD COHEN (B. 1934)

Leonard Cohen was already a well-reviewed poet and the author of two novels (one, *Beautiful Losers,* was singled out as "the most revolting book ever written in Canada") when he decided, at the rather advanced age of thirty-three, to try his hand as a singer/ songwriter. Though his sepulchral croak of a voice and monotone delivery may make you wonder how he ever got a record contract, that's a fleeting concern. Of far more interest are his literate lyrics and the dark romanticism he wraps around himself like a scarf. Together, they've inspired pretty much every sensitive, alienated teenager who decided to vent his pain through rock 'n' roll in the past forty years. He may never have achieved the fame of Bob Dylan, but Cohen is the dark horse folkie every rocker has a soft spot for. As U2's Edge has said of him, in the documentary *I'm Your Man,* "[He is] the man coming down from the mountaintop with tablets of stone having been up there talking to the angels."

The religious analogy is apt; it's the rare Cohen song that doesn't wield a biblical reference, though as a Jew growing up in the then overwhelmingly Catholic **Montreal**, his heightened sensitivity is understandable. Cohen's other preoccupations are love and sex, not always in that order, and they're woven throughout the album like sinuous ribbons. As a ladies' man, Cohen is a fatalist. "Suzanne," the opener and probably his best-known song, is full of gentle longing for a friend's wife (which is why he touched her "perfect body" with nothing more corporeal than his mind). "Teachers" and "So Long, Marianne" are poignant evocations of loss ("I'm cold as a new razor blade"), while "Master Song" brims with shivery intensity for some disturbing, if ambiguous, betrayal. All these are played out against a low-key boho wall of sound—which has held up surprisingly well—courtesy of producer John Simon.

Many of these songs turned out to be Cohen signatures, along with the later "Chelsea Hotel No. 2," his self-deprecating kiss-and-tell about having sex with Janis Joplin, and "Hallelujah," which has been covered by fans Rufus Wainwright and Jeff Buckley. But Cohen was never a very satisfactory rock star. After respectable sales for *The Songs of Leonard Cohen,* his numbers tapered off. At one point, his U.S. label refused to put out any more albums, because they didn't sell. And in the late '90s he disappeared into a Buddhist monastery for a while. But his influence, like his coterie of hard-core fans, has never waned.

ELECTRIC WARRIOR (1971),
T. REX

Though his pal David Bowie is more often thought of as the "Prettiest Star" of the early-'70s **glam rock** scene, Marc Bolan (who played guitar on the song's 1970 recording) gave him a run for his lip gloss. The elfin, androgynous Bolan, born Mark Feld

in markedly un-glam East London, favored tight shirts open to the waist and formfitting velvet trousers, and he liked to crown his Pre-Raphaelite curls with a top hat (the last a look later appropriated by Slash of Guns N' Roses). But Bolan wasn't just another photogenic, glitter-dusted face: With his band, T. Rex, he made some of the funkiest, sexiest, most gong-banging music ever committed to vinyl.

Marc Bolan's fey looks and extravagantly androgynous fashion sense had a huge impact on glam rock style.

Not without a false start, though. In the late '60s, Tyrannosaurus Rex (Bolan and percussionist Mickey Finn), as they were then known, were Donovan-esque hippie minstrels, obsessed with hobbits and mythical maidens. It was only when Bolan plugged in his guitar and put aside the Tolkien that his true identity as a rock provocateur emerged. It's a transformation alluded to in both *Electric Warrior*'s title and its cover image, which shows Bolan, guitar in hand, standing before a bank of amplifiers.

T. Rex had already scored a string of hits in the U.K. ("Twentieth Century Boy," "Children of the Revolution"), but Bolan was determined to crack the American charts. His strategy was to beef up the band's sound by adding bass player Steve Currie and drummer Bill Legend to the lineup, a sonic expansion that's evident from the opening notes of the first track, the gloriously sultry "Mambo Sun." The song's enticement to croon "beneath the bebop moon" is irresistible and slides you right into Bolan's sex-drenched world. The melodic raunchiness continues with the lusty, foot-stomping "Jeepster," which ends with an unequivocal "I'm going to suck you." By the time the thumping bass followed by the trill of piano keys opens "Bang a Gong (Get It On)"—this is an album that demands you turn up the sound—you're hooked; you want to be the "dirty, sweet" girl with the "diamond star halo" Bolan's panting after.

The song was T. Rex's only hit in the U.S., and remains their best-known effort on this side of the Atlantic. But in the U.K., and among the legions of musicians—everyone from Bowie to **punk** upstarts like the Ramones—who cite Bolan as an influence, he's the star he always wanted to be. Like all good rock stars, he died young, in a car crash just two weeks before his thirtieth birthday.

HORSES (1975), PATTI SMITH (B. 1946)

Even if all that existed of *Horses* was the cover art, it would have made Patti Smith an instant icon. The stark black-and-white photo, taken by Robert Mapplethorpe, shows her in all her skinny, shaggy-haired, androgynous glory, defiantly staring down anyone who'd dare to question her conviction that rock 'n' roll is the ultimate form of protest.

Smith, who at sixty-plus is still performing, is one of rock's most singular artists, and *Horses,* the album that introduced her to the world, is one of its milestones. It's widely perceived as the harbinger of **punk** (it beat the Ramones' debut effort to the punch by five months) and has been cited as an influence by everyone from the Talking Heads and REM to Courtney Love and PJ Harvey. But Smith didn't set out to be a punk heroine. She'd come to New York in 1967 to be a poet, like her idol, the nineteenth-century French symbolist Arthur Rimbaud (whom she insists was the first rock star). It was while rooming with her best friend Mapplethorpe at the Chelsea Hotel* that she met Lenny Kaye, whom she asked to play guitar at her poetry readings. They were eventually joined by guitarist Ivan Kral, drummer Jay Dee Daugherty, and pianist Richard Sohl, and it's this ensemble, under the name the Patti Smith Group, that recorded *Horses,* with former Velvet Undergrounder John Cale at the mixing board.

The album has one of the most notorious opening lines in rock: "Jesus died for somebody's sins, but not mine." It's the introductory salvo of Smith's poem "Oath," an ode to "positive anarchy" that slowly builds into an incandescent, raw-voiced cover of Van Morrison's raunchy '60s classic "Gloria." After that, *Horses* really starts defying expectations—its status as the iconoclastic beacon for a generation of DIY musical rebels stems not from three-chord, two-minute songs, but from its sheer audacity. Though the band sounds suitably unschooled, a result of playing live together in the studio with hardly any overdubs, the album's twin peaks are the spoken-word pieces "Birdland" and "Land," each of which clocks in at over nine minutes. The former is about a child who imagines his father is flying away in a UFO, while the latter is about a sexually charged encounter between two boys that morphs into a delirious send-up of dances like the Watusi; both are rife with Smith's trademark social commentary.

Horses was a critical success and sold modestly well, but, apart from the 1978 single "Because the Night," which she cowrote with Bruce Springsteen, Smith has never had the commercial success to match her industry-wide influence.

PARALLEL LINES (1978), BLONDIE

By the late 1970s, fans had taken to wearing buttons that read "Blondie is a group!" The defensive note was warranted: Blondie

---

* Though it can't be considered one of the Ten Chicest Hotels in the World, the rather threadbare Chelsea Hotel, on Twenty-third Street in Manhattan, has impeccable musical, literary, and artistic credentials. Everyone from **Simone de Beauvoir** and **Jean-Paul Sartre** to **Leonard Cohen** have called it home. More notoriously, it's where Sex Pistol Sid Vicious killed his girlfriend Nancy Spungeon.

may have been a sextet—singer Debbie Harry, her boyfriend Chris Stein on guitar, drummer Clem Burke, keyboard player Jimmy Destri, bass player Nigel Harrison, and guitarist Frank Infante— but two-tone bottle-blond Harry was always the band's focal point. The former *Playboy* bunny's potent blend of Old Hollywood– meets–**new wave** glamour and come-hither sexuality—somewhere, a young Madonna Ciccone was taking notes—made her the undisputed queen of the downtown Manhattan scene and was a driving factor in Blondie's success.

But then, Harry wasn't ever content to be the token chick in the band. Her high cheekbones and slinky dresses may have helped her take center stage, but she held on to it by virtue of her sexual confidence and sly sense of humor. It's a pose that's in full blossom on the cover of *Parallel Lines,* which has a pouting, white-clad Harry standing in front of her black-suited, skinny-necktied bandmates. They allegedly hated it, but its **pop art** graphicness perfectly conveys the album's blend of sweet pop, **punk** edge, and glossy sophistication.

Though they'd been one of the earliest new wave acts to play New York's legendary CBGB club and had released two well-received albums, it wasn't until *Parallel Lines* that Blondie became major stars. It couldn't have been otherwise: From its opening track, the jangly, insistent "Hanging on the Telephone," *Parallel Lines* is new wave bliss, shifting effortlessly from one song to the next. "One Way or Another" is the album's hardest rocker, while "Sunday Girl," a paean to the neighborhood belle, is a showcase for Harry's cool liquid vocals, and "Pretty Baby" shimmers with girl-group optimism. But it's the disco-inflected "Heart of Glass" that was the album's monster hit and the song that made Blondie, already fêted in Europe, famous back home. Though Burke was supposedly dismayed by producer Mike Chapman's finessing of what was originally a James Brown–style number, the song rides on his impeccable timing.

Blondie went on to have several more hits, including "Atomic," "Rapture," a rap-rock cross-pollination that's credited with introducing **hip-hop** to a white audience, and "Call Me," the theme song to *American Gigolo* (that and the Armani tailoring are the best things about the film), before breaking up in 1983 and then re-forming again fifteen years later. But they never again reached the consummate faultlessness of *Parallel Lines.*

RAISING HELL (1986), RUN-DMC

Run-DMC's third album catapulted them out of the musical fringe that rap was then relegated to and into the mainstream. The triple-platinum *Raising Hell* went all the way to number one on *Billboard*'s **R&B/hip-hop** chart and peaked at number six on the *Billboard* 200, making the three rappers from Hollis, Queens—Joseph "DJ Run" Simmons (brother of hip-hop mogul/Phat Farm CEO Russell Simmons), Darryl "D.M.C." McDaniels, and Jason "Jam-Master Jay" Mizell—first national and then global stars. In the process, it established hip-hop as a musical genre that white America could no longer ignore.

Today, the album's considered an old-school classic, packed with influential tracks from start to finish. As Chuck D of Public Enemy wrote in *Rolling Stone*'s tribute to the five hundred greatest artists of all time (Run-DMC came in at number forty-eight), "It's my favorite album of all time . . . Jay-Z, OutKast, Black Star, the Roots—everyone in hip-hop today can be traced back to Run-DMC."

Easing *Raising Hell*'s crossover success was its catchy incorpora-tion of rock riffs—not a new strategy for the trio, but one that producer Rick Rubin took to inspired heights, particularly on "It's Tricky," which sampled The Knack's "My Sharona," and, of course, the gleefully slick "Walk This Way," which took the stadium staple and gave it an urban jolt. The song not only brought Run-DMC a new fan base, it reinvigorated Aerosmith's own sagging street cred (to say nothing of their record sales). *Raising Hell*'s other highlights include a say-it-loud reworking of James Brown's "Proud to Be Black," which presaged the Afrocentric rap of the late '80s, and the song that sold a million pairs of sneakers—and presaged rap's logo obsession—"My Adidas."

"My Adidas" eventually scored Run-DMC an endorsement deal from the footwear manufacturer, a fashion twist that's as much a part of Run-DMC lore as their music. The group's pioneering dress sense was as influential as their pounding drum-machine beats and high-decibel delivery. Though they were from the rela-tively suburban New York City borough of Queens, their style was urban: jeans, logo-ed sportswear, spick-n-span kicks. It was a far cry from the disco-inspired outfits of earlier hip-hop artists like

Grandmaster Flash and provided the blueprint for the modern rapper uniform, just as their unambiguous, cross-armed stance on the album's sleeve became the attitude to cop.

SURFER ROSA (1988), THE PIXIES

Now that the Internet has obliterated the underground by exposing everything in about two minutes, it's easy to find cool music to load onto your iPod. But back in the dark days of 1988, before Nirvana released *Nevermind* and made alt-rock an essential category in every record store in every mall in North America, it wasn't so easy. The world was dominated by hair metal and Madonna, and if they weren't your idea of, well, Nirvana, you spent a lot of time searching out an alternative. Salvation came in the form of the Pixies, a Boston quartet whose blistering hybrid of hard core and surf rock was the impetus for **grunge**.

The Pixies formed in 1986, when anthropology student Black Francis (known to his parents as Charles Michael Kitridge Thompson IV) dropped out of college and persuaded his pal Joey Santiago to do the same. They took out an ad for a female bassist that specified, "Must like Hüsker Du and Peter Paul and Mary," and hired the only woman who replied, Kim Deal (who sometimes called herself Mrs. John Murphy). Deal recruited her drummer friend Dave Lovering, and the four started gigging.

Surfer Rosa, the band's first full-length LP, was released two years later. The arresting cover art—a topless flamenco dancer posed against a wall with a crucifix on it—is a warning of what's to come: ominous stream-of-consciousness lyrics, some in English, some in Spanish, about Old Testament violence, incest, mental illness, and voyeurism, all played out against a wall of sinewy guitars, stinging bass, and insistent drums that manage to be simultaneously abrasive and melodic. Thompson alternately whispers and howls on songs like the stop-and-go "Bone Machine" and "Break My Body," while Deal's breathy voice is the perfect counterpart to what's become the Pixies anthem, "Gigantic."

Though the Pixies were one of the most influential bands of the late '80s and early '90s—Kurt Cobain said that "Smells Like Teen

Spirit" was his attempt to write a Pixies song—by the time the movement they helped launch hit its stride, the fissures that split the band up in 1993 were already apparent. As Frank Black, Thompson went on to tour and record with his band, the Catholics, while Deal formed the Breeders and released a string of critically acclaimed albums (she even prompted her own pop ode, the Dandy Warhols' "Cool as Kim Deal"). But it was the Pixies' sold-out reunion tour in 2004 that excited the most attention, and gave fans an excuse to debate whether *Surfer Rosa* or its cleaner-sounding follow-up, *Doolittle* (1989), represented the band's zenith. Both are brilliant, but it's *Surfer Rosa*'s visceral roar that kick-started alt-rock.

HEAVEN OR LAS VEGAS (1990), THE COCTEAU TWINS

The Cocteau Twins, a Scottish trio who must hold some sort of record for reviews that use the word "ethereal," are the aural equivalent of mood-enhancing drugs—they didn't write songs so much as they crafted soundscapes to get lost in. Their dreamy melody-building reached its most coherent expression in *Heaven or Las Vegas,* an album that chugs along in a friendly fog of chewy bass lines, chiming guitars, and gossamer vocals that make the rest of the world seem thousands of miles away.

The Twins were born when guitarist Robin Guthrie and bassist Will Heggie (who was later replaced by Simon Raymonde), old school friends, spotted Liz Fraser dancing at a disco in the small town of Grangemouth, Scotland. Reasoning that if she could sing half as well as she danced she was just what they needed to round out their band, they asked her to join them. It was a brilliant choice: Fraser's delicate, buoyant voice is the fairy dust that adds magic to the Twins' lush waves of sound. With its ululations and flutters, it's not exactly a great method of conveying lyrics—*Heaven* is one of the only Twins records in which the words are anywhere near intelligible—but as an added layer of texture, it's gorgeous.

The band was quickly signed to 4AD Records, a British label whose self-appointed mission was to promote music that was "timeless, free of any trend, movement or era," making it the perfect home for a band that didn't sound like anything else. The group's first few releases won them a devoted following, but they chafed under the "fey Victoriana" tag their melancholic song titles ("When Mama Was Moth," "Glass Candle Grenades") and ghosts-and-lace cover image earned them. The gloom was jettisoned for *Heaven:* The sleeve depicts a crest of neon arcing a pulsing red-and-blue sky and the attitude is altogether more upbeat, as though Fraser, Guthrie, and Raymonde were listening to Abba and eating strawberry ice cream in between takes. "Cherry-Coloured Funk" is a warm kiss of a song, while the title track is pure, unadulterated ear candy. The whole album moves along at an unhurried pace, pausing for the high-note fireworks of "Fotzepolitic" and the enigmatic, lovelorn "Road, River and Rail" before winding up at the winsome, hum-along farewell of "Frou-Frou Foxes in Midsummer Fire." At just over thirty-seven and a half minutes, the trip's too short. When it's all over, the only thing to do is press play and get lost again.

69 LOVE SONGS (1999), THE MAGNETIC FIELDS

It's safe to say that more songs have been written about love—wanting it, finding it, blowing it—than any other topic under the sun. It's equally safe to say that none of them are quite like the ones you'll find on *69 Love Songs,* a three-disk set from weary romantic Stephin Merritt and his main project, The Magnetic Fields (which is named for a **dada** prose poem by André Breton). The rest of the band consists of banjo player/lead guitarist/mandolin player John Woo, percussionist/pianist/occasional vocalist Claudia Gonson, and cellist/flutist Sam Davol.

What makes *69 Love Songs* unique is its tremendous musical and topical span. Using an array of instruments that includes accordions, harpsichords, and ukuleles, Merritt has assembled a virtual anthology of twentieth-century pop music, from Kurt Weill through to '60s girl groups and on to '80s synth. He's taken every cliché he's ever heard, extracted its maddening brilliance, and spun it into a mischievous new interpretation that sounds both poignantly familiar and toe-tappingly new. From the tender, honky-

MUSICAL GENRES DEMYSTIFIED

- **Electronica** covers a wide range of styles, but it's generally defined as electronic music that's intended for home listening, not clubbing. In other words, music to take drugs to. • **Glam rock**, a.k.a. glitter rock, was at its spangled peak in the early '70s, when bands like T. Rex and the New York Dolls were bending genders and guitar licks. • Fashion-wise, Seattle-born, flannel-shirt-wearing **grunge** is glam rock's polar opposite. Musically, this early-'90s style was inspired by heavy metal and punk rock. • **Hip-hop**, which is built on rapping and DJing, first emerged in New York City in the early 1970s, but its climb to industry domination didn't begin until the late 1980s. • **Mashup** digitally combines the music from one song with the vocals of another. As it borrows liberally from many genres, it's also known as bastard pop. • Since they were both products of the mid-1970s, the term **new wave** is often used interchangeably with punk, but it's more polished, musically more experimental, and lyrically more sophisticated. • **Punk** came first, and it's harder, faster, and very definitely pissed-off. • The term **R&B,** or rhythm and blues, was first coined in the 1940s, and, as the name suggests, it's influenced by blues, jazz, and gospel. Thanks to artists like Beyoncé, it's now the most popular form of music in the U.S. • **Reggae** originated in Jamaica in the late 1960s. It's played in 4/4 time and usually has a pretty simple structure, sometimes with no more than two chords in a song. • Purists divide it into multiple subgenres, but **techno,** which traces its roots to mid-1980s Detroit, is a generic term for electronic dance music.

tonk- colored "Papa Was a Rodeo" to the quasi-improvised beatnik doodlings of "Love Is Like Jazz," his musical chameleon act is a continual delight.

Every manifestation of love is covered, from the woman whose boyfriend has moved across the country to write a novel ("Come Back From San Francisco") to the Rockette reminiscing about a

Parisian dalliance with an army officer ("The Night You Can't Remember"). But it's Merritt's songwriting, delivered in his drowsy drawl, that gives *69 Love Songs* its bite. He's the Cole Porter of contemporary urban bohemia, lending his inventive wordplay to both divinely silly ditties like "Let's Pretend We're Bunny Rabbits" ("Let's pretend we're bunny rabbits / let's do it all day long / Let abbots, Babbitts and Cabots / say Mother Nature's wrong") and sardonic breakup songs like "I Don't Want to Get Over You" ("I could make a career of being blue / I could dress in black and read Camus/but I don't want to get over you"). From brokenhearted misanthrope to blissed-out innocent, Merritt adopts one persona after another. The continual role-playing means you never really get an idea of who he is, but the mystery is part of his appeal.

This was the album that brought The Magnetic Fields mainstream attention, but even long-term, die-hard fans, the kind who want to keep a band all to themselves, can't begrudge its success. *69 Love Songs* is not just about love, it's about loving music.

TEN FILMS
TO KNOW ABOUT

FILM IS THE CLOSEST contemporary culture comes to having a lingua franca, so it tends to come up a lot in conversation. As with any language, mastering the basics is the first step toward fluency in its finer points. From the erotic tension of *Pandora's Box* to *Chinatown's* noir beauty, these films are all classics that every cineast is conversant with.

PANDORA'S BOX (1929),
G. W. PABST (1885–1967)

Louise Brooks's career was tantalizingly brief. She arrived in Hollywood in 1927 and made the last of her twenty-five films, most of which featured her as a bit player, by 1938, after which she disappeared from public view. Nevertheless, her shiny, black-bobbed image is one of the most enduring of the twentieth century. Almost eighty years after her appearance as Lulu, the amoral heroine of *Pandora's Box,* and the role she's most closely identified with, her gamine erotic presence is irresistible. When filmmakers want to suggest that a character is a volatile mix of girlish naïveté and sexual dynamism—as did Jean-Luc Godard in *Vivre sa vie* (1962) or Quentin Tarantino in *Pulp Fiction* (1994)—they inevitably give her Brooks's signature coif.

The choice of an unknown American actress to play a cherished symbol of Weimar decadence—the film was based loosely on a hit play by Frank Wedekind—caused an uproar in Germany, but Pabst was so convinced that Brooks was his Lulu, a call girl whose raison d'être is the hedonistic pursuit of pleasure, that he cast her before they ever met, based purely on her potent screen presence. But Brooks wasn't one for come-hither looks and heaving bosoms. Small and slight, she plays Lulu as a childish innocent with a grown-up woman's desires, a performance that makes Marlene Dietrich look like an over-accessorized drag queen.

Lulu's unthinking sensuality is what first attracts Schön, the wealthy publisher who marries her, though it doesn't take long for him to realize his folly: At the wedding reception, the bride snuggles up to both his son and a predatory countess (one of the screen's first lesbians). As soon as they're alone, the disgusted Schön presses a gun into her hand and orders her to commit suicide so that their reputations can be saved. Lulu, naturally, refuses. In the ensuing struggle, the gun goes off and Schön is killed. Lulu's found guilty of the murder, but her besotted admirers arrange her escape. She flees across Europe, eventually landing in a shabby flat in London. It's here, out of the fog, that her nemesis appears: Jack the Ripper (Gustav Diessl). She invites him up, and, though he's temporarily swayed by her intoxicating presence, the inevitable happens. It's a climax best described by Brooks in her memoir, *Lulu in Hollywood:* "It is Christmas Eve and she is about to receive the gift that has been her dream since childhood. Death by a sexual maniac."

Thanks to its raw sexuality, *Pandora's Box* is one of the most exceptional films of the silent era and Brooks one of its most intriguing figures. A cult figure in Europe since the 1950s, she was almost forgotten altogether in her native country. It wasn't until 1979, when Kenneth Tynan published "The Girl in the Black Helmet," a mash note disguised as a profile in *The New Yorker*— even at seventy-three, Brooks was a charmer—that she got the recognition she deserves.

ALL ABOUT EVE (1950),
JOSEPH L. MANKIEWICZ (1909-1993)

"Fasten your seat belts—it's going to be a bumpy night!" Bette Davis delivers the most famous line in *All About Eve* with obvious relish, and you can't blame her. Margo Channing, an aging theater star who wears drama like perfume, is the role of a lifetime, and Davis obviously loved every minute of playing her. Her nomination for best actress (she lost to Judy Holliday, who won for *Born Yesterday*) was just one of fourteen the film received.

The film's story is familiar enough: protégée tries to steal star's thunder, with varying results. What sets *Eve* apart is its tart, sophisticated dialogue. From the opening scene, a theatrical awards dinner for newcomer Eve Harrington (Anne Baxter) narrated by the critic Addison DeWitt (George Sanders), you know you're in for a good time. "My native habitat is the theater," he purrs. "In it I toil not, neither do I spin. I am a critic and commentator. I am as essential to the theater as ants to a picnic, as the boll weevil to a cotton field. . . ."

The flashback story line then rewinds to Eve and Margo's first meeting, a disaster-in-waiting unwittingly engineered by Margo's best friend. At first, everyone is charmed by Eve's Oliver Twist routine. Everyone, that is, except Margo's faithful maid/dresser, Birdie (Thelma Ritter), whose reaction is a narrow-eyed "Everything but the bloodhounds snappin' at her rear." Before long, Eve is ensconced in Margo's household, bringing her breakfast, running her errands, and generally making herself indispensable, chores she intersperses with self-deprecating comments like "I'm less than nobody." But the slavish devotion, as any thirteen-year-old girl could tell you, is just an act. What Eve really wants is Margo's life. It's once Margo gets wise to her that *All About Eve* really gets rolling. Mankiewicz, who both wrote and directed the film, was a master of bitchy repartee, and the script is barbed with viperish put-downs. A case in point: When Eve tries to end her affair with Addison by throwing open the door of her hotel room and ordering him out, he sneers, "You're too short for that gesture."

With lines like that, it's no wonder that *All About Eve* continues to be quoted. It's also renowned for Marilyn Monroe's screen debut, in the scene in which Davis gives her dramatic turbulence warning.

It's a small part, but Monroe holds her own. She plays Addison's date, Miss Caswell, "a graduate of the Copacabana School of Dramatic Arts." When he points her in the direction of a perspiring, dyspeptic producer, she sighs, "Why do they always look like scared rabbits?" Given her unhappy life, it's a sadly telling line.

RASHÔMON (1950),
AKIRA KUROSAWA (1910-1998)

The first line of *Rashômon* is "I just don't understand." The speaker is a woodcutter (Takashi Shimura) who has heard three different accounts of the same crime and can't reconcile them. His words, forgotten five minutes later, prove to be prophetic.

Rashômon is the film that introduced Japanese cinema to the West, where it was an instant hit, winning both the Golden Lion at the Venice Film Festival and the Academy Award for best foreign film. As even people who haven't seen it know, it's about a situation that is recounted by different witnesses, none of whom agree on what happened. The film is such a perfect summation of this quandary that its title has become part of the English language—as with Joseph Heller's *Catch-22,* there's simply no better way of expressing the situation it describes. It's even achieved that bellwether of pop-culture relevance, a reference on *The Simpsons:*

> **Marge:** You liked *Rashômon.*
> **Homer:** That's not how *I* remember it.

The film opens in a torrential downpour. Two men, the woodcutter and a priest (Minoru Chiaki), have taken shelter at Kyoto's Rashômon Gate. A third joins them and asks what they're talking about. They explain: A woman traveler (Machiko Kyô) has been raped by a notorious bandit named Tajômaru (Toshirô Mifune), and her samurai husband (Masayuki Mori) killed. The woodcutter discovered the husband's body and reported it to the authorities. Both men have just been listening to the accounts of the crime's three witnesses—the bandit, the wife, and the dead samurai, who spoke through a medium—to the court (this being cinematic twelfth-century Japan, the dead can apparently testify in this manner). In a series of flashbacks, we learn that each one has a completely different story, and each one confesses to the murder. Finally, the woodcutter admits that he saw the entire thing, and he tells yet another version of the story. Because he wasn't involved in the crime, his version would appear to be credible. But it turns out that he stole the woman's valuable dagger—which is why he didn't come forward earlier—so he's no more reliable than the others.

Who's telling the truth? It's impossible to know. *Rashômon* depends on our credulity as viewers. We keep watching because we think that at some point we're going figure out what really went on in that clearing in the woods. But that never happens. Instead, we're left with four equally plausible scenarios and no way of knowing which one of them is factual. Morever, Kurosawa has us wondering if we can ever again trust what we see.

VERTIGO (1958), ALFRED HITCHCOCK (1899-1980)

Of all Alfred Hitchcock's films, none combines the stylish tension and creeping Freudian undertones that *Vertigo* revels in. From the Saul Bass opening titles to the shattering denouement, it's pure class all the way. Its story line traverses the minefield that lies, as Calvin Klein described decades later, "between love and madness"— i.e., erotic obsession, and though the hints of fetishism and necrophilia didn't sit well with late-1950s audiences, it's now widely regarded as Hitchcock's best film. It's certainly his most personal: The director would become infatuated with the (usually blond) actresses he cast, insisting they dress and behave in ways that conformed to his ideas of beauty and sexual appeal, a scenario that's played out to chilling effect in the film. Like Hitch, his hero (James Stewart) likes ice queens with molten centers, and he'll go to great lengths to get what he wants.

Stewart plays John "Scottie" Ferguson, a San Francisco detective forced into early retirement due to the sudden onset of acrophobia (fear of heights) that manifests itself as acute vertigo. Restless and bored, he readily agrees when his old college buddy Gavin Elster contacts him and asks him to follow his wife, Madeleine

(Kim Novak), who's been acting strangely lately. It's a fateful decision—the instant Scottie sees the enigmatic blond, he's smitten. He falls in love with Madeleine and believes she feels the same way about him. Then, one day, tragedy strikes: She plunges to her death from the top of a bell tower, an accident Scottie's vertigo prevents him from averting. But Madeleine, it turns out, was not who she seemed—and she may not be dead. Scottie, who's in the grip of an erotic compulsion so profound that he seems unaware of anything else, sets out to find her. When he finally tracks her down, she turns out to be a dark-haired hoyden in a tight sweater named Judy (Novak again), who acted the part of Elster's wife as part of the cover-up of her murder. Scottie moves in with a vengeance, transforming her, with the help of a team of beauticians and one of the city's finer department stores, into the sophisticated woman he fell in love with. Unfortunately, no one ever warned him of the dangers of playing god; it's a situation that can only end in disaster.

Vertigo is a quintessential example of art that is ahead of its time. Upon its release, it was dismissed as melodramatic nonsense. Fifty years on, the film's darkness and sexual malaise resonate with a profoundness that its early detractors couldn't have imagined.

8 ½ (1963), FEDERICO FELLINI (1920-1993)

Perhaps because it's a film about a director trying to make a film, *8 ½* regularly tops many directors' best-movie lists. But Federico Fellini's autobiographical tale of a man who's lost his inspiration is more than just an exercise in professional solipsism—it's a free-flowing rumination on the nature of art and creativity.

Like his previous effort *La Dolce Vita* (1960), a chronicle of Rome by night that features the memorable sight of Anita Ekberg cavorting in the Fountain of Trevi, *8 ½* (the title refers to the number of films Fellini had made to date; the half is a segment of a longer collaboration) abandons the **neorealism** of earlier productions. But where *La Dolce Vita* flirted with fantasy, *8 ½* takes it to bed.

The film opens with an image of suffocation. Guido Anselmi (Marcello Mastroianni), a successful director who's clearly based on Fellini, is trapped in a traffic jam. He can't breathe, but no one seems to care; they just stare impassively from inside their own cars. Then Guido breaks free and floats high above the earth, only to be yanked to the ground again by his associates, who in the real world are badgering him to get to work on the sci-fi epic he's lost all interest in. Along with his wife (Anouk Aimée) and mistress (Sandra Milo), they follow him to a resort near Rome, where most of the film takes place. Much of the action, however, takes place in Guido's head, where he retreats whenever his uncooperative screenwriter, testy producer, and various needy actors and actresses try to pin him down.

His baroque dreamworld is a mix of memories (some real, others pure invention) and dreams, all vividly imagined by Fellini, who weaves them seamlessly into the narrative. Guido seeks comfort from his dead father, who leads him into the graveyard where he's buried; there, his mother kisses him and turns into his wife. His father, meanwhile, turns out to be his producer. Later, in a restaurant where Guido and his wife are seated near his mistress, he drifts into a famous fantasy in which he lives in a house with all the women in his life, holding them at bay with a ringmaster's whip. He finds solace from his floundering in the angelic support of his muse (Claudia Cardinale), a figure who's more satisfying as a figment of his imagination; when she finally appears, she's a dud.

Guido never makes his film, which is where his resemblance to Fellini ends. He's out of ideas, exhausted by the very idea of making a movie. But Fellini had no such problem: *8½*, which won the Academy Award for best foreign film, is considered his greatest achievement.

JULES ET JIM (1962), FRANÇOIS TRUFFAUT (1932–1984)

Jules et Jim sweeps you straight into its joyride. The film opens to the sound of a carousel, and its first scenes have the same jerky charm and

The femme fatale as an adolescent boy—Jeanne Moreau in the French new wave classic Jules et Jim, *in which she played one of the most maddening women in film.*

speed. It's bohemian Paris, 1912. A breathless voice-over introduces us to a shy Austrian writer named Jules (Oskar Werner), who quickly becomes inseparable friends with the French Jim (Henri Serre), who's also a writer but more of an extrovert. They go everywhere together. Then they meet the slightly mad, mercurial Catherine (Jeanne Moreau), who keeps a bottle of sulfuric acid in her room "for the eyes of men who tell lies." Jules is smitten. Though they've always shared everything, including their girlfriends, he says, "But not this one, okay, Jim?" Jim nods, and the charmed twosome becomes a charmed threesome. In one scene, Catherine dresses like a boy with a cartoon mustache painted on her cheeks and they lark around Montmartre. Another time, they go to see a new play. Jules and Jim are critical of it, but Catherine admires its headstrong heroine. To prove her point, she suddenly jumps into the Seine. Her leap, says the omnipresent narrator, "strikes Jim like lightning." Now both friends are in love with Catherine, and the film's die is cast. Though she marries Jules, he's too plodding and kind to keep her attention for long. When he tells her he understands her, she replies that she doesn't want to be understood. She takes the slightly more dashing Jim as a lover, but he tires of her machinations.

Though the film is named for the two men, Catherine is its endlessly spinning center. The only true free spirit of the trio—even when we first see Jules and Jim living out their bohemian dreams, they seem a bit stolid—she's impossible to categorize. One minute she's a feminist, the next she can't live without a man. She's a doting mother who abandons her daughter, a proponent of free love who insists on fidelity. When she finally drives herself and Jim off a bridge, you understand Jules's sense of relief.

A landmark of the **French new wave**, *Jules et Jim* was made when François Truffaut was still in his twenties. But although it has all the new wave's youthful tricks—rapid scene changes, fluid camera work, an insistence on reminding viewers that they're having a cinematic experience—it also has the empathy of experience. That may be because the novel Truffaut based his script on was written by an older man looking back at his youth. Henri-Pierre Roché, a writer with ties to the **dada** movement, based his story on the real-life love triangle that existed between himself, **Marcel Duchamp**, and the American artist Beatrice Wood.

FACES (1968),
JOHN CASSAVETES (1929–1989)

If John Cassavetes didn't exactly invent indie filmmaking, with highly personal, slice-of-life movies like *Faces* he demonstrated that there was an option to following Hollywood's rules, which by the mid-1960s were feeling increasingly out of touch with reality. In the process, he laid down the genre's aesthetic ground rules: jumpy, handheld camera work, low-fi locations, improvised or quasi-improvised acting, realistic dialogue, and gritty subject matter, all characteristics that *Faces,* which went on to garner three Academy Award nominations, brims with.

Cassavetes started out as an actor (he's Rosemary's egomaniacal but charming satanist husband in *Rosemary's Baby*), a trade he returned to whenever he needed money to finance his film projects, which was pretty much constantly. *Faces* was no exception—he wrote and directed it over an eight-month period in 1965, then spent three years trying to find a distributor.

The black-and-white film follows an eighteen-hour period in the winding down of a marriage. Richard (John Marley) and Maria (Lynn Carlin) Forst are middle-class, middle-aged Angelenos. He's a frustrated businessman; she's a bored housewife; their conversations consist of bouts of nervous laughter punctuated with pauses to mix fresh drinks. They're the kind of brittle couple Joan Didion wrote about in her definitive exposé of the underbelly of sun-kissed California, "Some Dreamers of the Golden Dream," published the same year *Faces* was released.

Richard comes home one night and announces that he wants a divorce, then heads out for a date with Jeannie (Gena Rowlands, Cassavetes's wife and artistic collaborator), a prostitute he's become enamored of. Maria, meanwhile, visits a go-go club with three of her friends, where they pick up a beatnik lothario (Seymour Cassel) named Chet. Many highballs later (alcohol is the only release these people seem to have), both Richard and Maria reach the same not-so-startling conclusion: Their unhappiness has more to do with their individual personal emptiness than with their incompatibility. Whether they'll do anything with this new knowledge is inconclusive; for them, this realization itself is a major breakthrough.

Faces' claustrophobic close-ups and long, meandering scenes don't always make for gripping viewing, but compared to many other films that were being made during the period—*The Sound of Music* and *Mary Poppins* were the top-grossing movies of 1965—it's bracingly authentic, a dollop of **cinema verité**. But its real legacy is its relaxed pacing, renegade camera work, and DIY spirit. For younger filmmakers such as Martin Scorsese and Francis Ford Coppola, *Faces* pointed the way forward.

Cassavetes's legacy also has a more personal note: The two children he and Rowlands had, Nick Cassavetes *(The Notebook)* and Zoë Cassavetes *(Men Make Women Crazy Theory, Broken English)*, are both directors.

CHINATOWN (1974), ROMAN POLANSKI (B. 1933)

Roman Polanski's last American film is impressive even by the standards of its era, when one great film after another *(Bonnie and Clyde, The Godfather)* was coming out of Hollywood. It's a gorgeously shot homage to **film noir**, that black-and-white genre that combined cynical private eyes, beautiful femmes fatales, and **Kafka**esque narratives. But *Chinatown* is no ordinary noir, just as Polanski is no ordinary director. A Holocaust survivor whose wife (Sharon Tate) and unborn child were murdered by the Manson family, Polanski had long been on intimate terms with the baser side of human nature. So when the film's villain, Noah Cross (John Huston), tries to explain away his incestuous relationship with his teenage daughter Evelyn by saying, "Most people never have to face the fact that in the right time and the right place they're capable of anything," you get the impression that Polanski knows exactly what he's talking about. Giving the line an extra frisson of menace is Polanski's own attraction to adolescent girls, which led to his arrest, four years after *Chinatown* was released, for allegedly having sex with a thirteen-year-old girl. Rather than face charges, he fled the U.S., and hasn't returned since.

The film's plotline is tortuous: Jack Nicholson stars as J. J. "Jake" Gittes, a former cop turned private investigator in 1930s Los Angeles. He's hired by a woman calling herself Evelyn Mulwray, who wants him to investigate her husband's infidelities. Jake obliges with photos of her husband and a young blond woman, which are subsequently published. All is not what it seems, however, and the real Evelyn Mulwray, née Cross (Faye Dunaway), soon arrives in Jake's office, lawyer in tow. But when Mulwray turns up dead, she enlists Jake to find his killer. At the same time, her father, who was Mulwray's former business partner, hires him to find the young blond. That's when things really get complicated. Jake finds himself investigating a political scandal that reaches to the upper echelons of L.A. society. Before it's over, Evelyn is dead and the young blond, who turns out to be Evelyn's daughter by her father (thus the famous "She's my daughter! She's my sister!" line), is handed over to Cross.

Evelyn's spectacular death—she's shot through the eye—is foreshadowed at several points in the script, most memorably when Jake notices a black spot in her eye. "It's a flaw in the iris," she says, with what turns out to be monumental understatement. In insisting on a tragic denouement, Polanski was defying screenwriter Robert Towne, who won the film's only Oscar. But given the director's morbid sensibility—darkness lurks just below the surface in his films—any other ending would have felt false.

PICNIC AT HANGING ROCK (1975), PETER WEIR (B. 1944)

With its hypnotic pace, virginal white-clad schoolgirls, and barely smothered sexual hysteria, *Picnic at Hanging Rock* suggests a Timotei

commercial crossed with a Gothic horror story. If that sounds baf-
fling, you're not alone; critics have often found it incomprehensible.
But if *Picnic at Hanging Rock* wasn't incomprehensible, there would
be no reason to watch it; it's a mystery whose entire point is that it's
a mystery, a paradox that makes it essential viewing for film buffs.

The narrative, however, is straightforward enough: On Saint
Valentine's Day, 1900, a group of Australian schoolgirls go for an
outing at Hanging Rock, a volcanic outcropping near their school.
Three of them, along with one of their teachers, disappear without
a trace. One girl is found a few days later but can't remember
anything of what took place. The others are never seen again. We
never learn what happened to them, and neither do any of the
other characters. That's it.

Except that isn't it at all. As Peter Weir makes clear, there's far
more to this girls' school, and this outing, than meets the eye. He
immediately establishes the film's atmosphere of budding sexuality
and undercurrent of erotic tension. The girls are seen exchanging
valentines and lacing each other's corsets prior to setting off on
their excursion. Before they leave, their headmistress, who obviously has some unresolved issues of her own, gives a bizarre speech
in which she describes the rock in unintentionally sexual terms.

The rock turns out to be a dark, uninviting colossus. Most of
the girls are happily oblivious to its strange power, but the ones
who set off to explore it seem compelled to do so; they're like
acolytes setting off for a ritual offering. Weir heightens the tension
by contrasting the rock's spookiness with gauzy, sun-dappled
cinematography and eerie panpipes. The combination of girlish
innocence and lurking disaster is stylishly hypnotic, a factor that
wasn't lost on later directors—Sofia Coppola's *The Virgin Suicides*
(1999), for one, another film about doomed young women,
borrows heavily from *Picnic at Hanging Rock.*

Even the characters who are unaffected by Hanging Rock find
themselves noticing odd things; their watches, for example, have all
stopped. Though Weir offers no more than hints of what's
happened to the girls, the suggestion is that it's something primal
that these buttoned-up Victorians simply can't comprehend, no
matter how many times they return to search for clues.

The film was based on Joan Lindsay's 1967 novel, which,
despite persistent rumors to the contrary, was completely fictional.

However, the original manuscript included a chapter that explained what happened to the girls. This was published as *The Secret of Hanging Rock* in 1987, two years after Lindsay's death. Her solution is that the girls and their teacher find an opening in the rock that's a portal into another dimension and crawl into it. It closes before the third girl can join them. While this mystical scenario may not satisfy viewers who want to know that something more horrific happened, it does fit in with the disconnect between the European arrivistes and the ancient continent they've settled, which was one of the book's central themes.

BREAKING THE WAVES (1996), LARS VON TRIER (B. 1956)

Watching *Breaking the Waves* is an emotionally grueling experience. It begins as a carnal love story, descends into the sort of melodrama and madness that most directors would run in horror from, and ends with an image of spiritual affirmation that, depending on your willingness to follow Lars von Trier on the course he has set, can be read as either beatific or sappy.

The Danish von Trier, who also wrote the film's script, is one of the most provocative filmmakers working today. He's notoriously eccentric, and his work, which disregards any notion of political correctness, can be hard to watch. *The Idiots* (1998), for example, features a group of people who pretend to be mentally handicapped in order to connect with their "inner idiot." He's a member of the avant-garde Dogma 95 movement, which aims to purify filmmaking from superfluous distractions like special effects and artificial lighting. Though *Breaking the Waves* doesn't follow all of Dogma 95's "Vows of Chastity"—it's set in the 1970s rather than the present, for one thing—it does display the movement's puritanical ethos.

The film centers on Bess McNeill (Emily Watson), a childlike innocent whose face shines with pure goodness. She lives in an isolated Calvinist community in the north of Scotland where even church bells are seen as frivolous. Her church elders consider her simpleminded and are not pleased by her decision to marry Jan

FILM GENRES AND WHAT THEY MEAN

• **B movies** were originally low-budget films intended for distribution as the supporting acts in a double feature. The term's now a byword for schlock. • The **blaxploitation** films of the early 1970s featured primarily black actors, badass urban environments, and plenty of sex and violence—especially if Pam Grier, the original Foxy Brown, was involved. • **Bollywood** refers to the Mumbai-based Hindi film industry, where melodramatic plots and spontaneous outbreaks of choreography are de rigueur. • **Cinema ver-ité**, or cinema of truth, combines the naturalistic style of documentary filmmaking with the narrative structure of scripted films. In other words, the actors don't look nearly as good as they do in Hollywood blockbusters. • **Film noir**, which means black film, flourished in Hollywood in the 1940s and '50s, when men were men and women were dames. These movies are generally crime dramas with ambiguous moral messages. • The films of the **French new wave**, which reached its apogee in the 1950s and '60s, were self-consciously cinematic, and placed an emphasis on the director as the "author" of his or her film. • **German expressionism**, with its villainous heroes and moody juxta-position of shadows and light, was the 1920s precursor to film noir. • **Hong Kong action** films combine the violence of action films with traditional Chinese storytelling. What they lack in original plots—betrayal and revenge are on an endless loop here—they make up for with gravity-defying stunts. • **Italian neorealism** flourished in the 1940s and early 1950s and dealt openly with the harsh economic and social conditions that Italy faced after the war. • The Italian **spaghetti westerns** of the 1960s were a subversive take on the good-guy-always-wins American western. They're also the reason Clint Eastwood has a career.

(Stellan Skarsgård), a Danish oil-rig worker. But Bess, who's a virgin, is so in love with Jan, and so eager to experience sex with him, that she locks the two of them in the bathroom at their wedding reception and announces, "You can love me now."

Bess is ecstatically happy with Jan, and the sheer physical rapture of their life together adds an extra dimension of tragedy to the events that follow. When Jan returns to his rig, she begs God to bring him home. He does come back, but only after an accident leaves him paralyzed from the neck down. In a harsh twist on their former relationship, the depressed and medicated Jan asks Bess to have sex with other men and then tell him about it. Believing this is the only thing that will save Jan's life, Bess agrees, and begins a dark odyssey of degrading sex that ends in her brutal death. In the next scene, Jan has miraculously recovered and is grieving his dead wife. Refusing to agree to a funeral in which Bess will be condemned to hell as a sinner, he steals her body and buries her at sea. The film ends with the pealing of bells, as Jan and his coworkers stare up into the heavens with wonder. If you've gone along with von Trier, then you can conclude that God was listening to Bess all along. If not, then the ringing of the bells may seem like just one more cruel invention.

FIVE FILMS
EVERY FASHION
FAN HAS SEEN

THOUGH NOT ALL THESE FILMS are about fashion, they're all unassailably stylish, hence their popularity with the professionally image-conscious. Two of the five, you'll note, are about fascism—a coincidence that no one who's worked in fashion would dismiss as purely accidental.

QUI-ÊTES-VOUS, POLLY MAGGOO? (1966), WILLIAM KLEIN (B. 1928)

Though difficult to track down, this stylized parody of the French fashion scene of the mid-'60s, directed by the American expat photographer William Klein, is worth the effort it takes to find it. Everyone in sight has a geometric Vidal Sassoon haircut, and the film's eyeliner budget must have been substantial. Dorothy McGowan, who plays the title character, a variation on the American naïf in Paris, was plucked from a gaggle of Beatles fans waiting to welcome the Fab Four to New York. She's the model of the moment, being trailed by a documentary camera crew. An inspired

Grayson Hall, meanwhile, plays a **Diana Vreeland**–like fashion editor. "He's re-created Woman!" she shrieks after viewing a designer's collection of sheet-metal dresses. "Well, I tried my best," he replies.

THE DAMNED (1969),
LUCHINO VISCONTI (1906–1976)

A family of German munitions manufacturers fall under the spell of National Socialism. Ingrid Thulin stars as the chic but unscrupulous Baroness von Essenbeck; Helmut Berger plays her son Martin, a murderous pedophile. She tries to use him as a pawn to advance her second husband's career, but both she and her husband end up being forced to commit suicide. That's about as cheery as this relentlessly grim study of the machinations of Nazism gets, but the Oscar-winning film's languid costumes and general air of decadence—it makes *Cabaret* look like a day at the seaside—have made it a fashion favorite. It had a *huge* influence on the vintage-clothing revival.

THE NIGHT PORTER (1974),
LILIANA CAVANI (B. 1933)

The poster for this controversial film—a topless Charlotte Rampling in a Nazi uniform—lets you know what you're in for. She plays Lucia, a former concentration-camp victim now married to an American opera conductor. On a visit to Vienna in 1957, they accidentally run into Lucia's lover/torturer from the concentration camp, Max (Dirk Bogarde), who is the night porter at their hotel. Max, an SS officer during the Third Reich, is preparing for his trial for war crimes; Lucia is the only living witness of his deeds. Contrary to the orders of Max's former SS colleagues, who want him to eliminate her, the two take up their obsessive, sadomasochistic relationship again. A stygian look at the nature of sexual transgression.

BELLE DE JOUR (1967),
LUIS BUÑUEL (1900-1983)

When the prissy 1960s lady look hit the runways a few years ago, fashion magazines were full of *Belle de Jour* references. As the film's heroine, Séverine, a young Parisian housewife with an ample clothing allowance, Catherine Deneuve was certainly the epitome of tasteful chic in head-to-toe **Yves Saint Laurent** (though it was Roger Vivier who made the iconic buckle flats she wears). The very correct clothes are a contrast to the story line: Unable to be intimate with her husband, Séverine secretly freelances at a high-class brothel, where she can live out her elaborate masochistic fantasies. What makes the film an erotic classic is director Luis Buñuel's understanding of human nature—he knew very well that sex begins in the mind.

GREY GARDENS (1975),
ELLEN HOVDE, ALBERT AND
DAVID MAYSLES, MUFFIE MEYER

This documentary about a dotty mother-and-daughter duo (none other than Jackie Onassis's aunt and cousin) and their myriad cats living out their days in the moldering family beach house on Long Island has launched a thousand fashion shoots. The two had lived together in semiseclusion since the mid-1950s, when Big Edie's husband abandoned the family and Little Edie, then an aspiring dancer, came home to look after her mother. The directors just let them do their thing, and it makes for fascinating viewing. Big Edie flips through old albums that document her pre–World War II heyday, while Little Edie philosophizes, wears her cardigan as a head scarf, and shows an admirable flair for accessorizing.

TEN ICONIC OBJECTS AND THEIR DESIGNERS

SOMETIMES A CHAIR is more than just something to sit on—it's a lifestyle statement, an avowal of personal taste, an affirmation of status. In other words, its form is as important as its function. The chairs—and tables and vases and computers—listed here are all celebrated examples of the meeting of these two main tenets of design.

HILL HOUSE CHAIR (1904), CHARLES RENNIE MACKINTOSH (1868-1928)

In contrast to the sinuous curves that **art nouveau** followed on the continent, its Scottish manifestation was stricter and altogether subtler. As practiced in Glasgow, a major center of art nouveau architecture and design, the blowsiness evident in Paris and Barcelona was reined in and tempered. Its foremost practitioner was Charles Rennie Mackintosh, who—along with his wife, Margaret MacDonald; Margaret's sister Frances MacDonald; and Frances's husband, Herbert MacNair—was one of The Four, a design collective whose influence spread far beyond Scotland. They

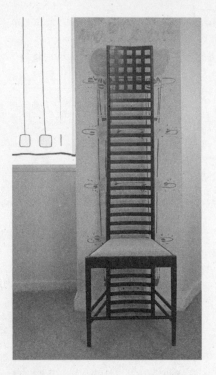

Charles Rennie Makintosh's Hill House chair

drew on a variety of inspirations for their work, including the proto-hippie arts and crafts movement, the medievalist Pre-Raphaelites, and traditional Scottish and Japanese art.

Although he trained as an architect, the prolific Mackintosh also worked in interior design, furniture, textiles, and metalwork. Variations on his signature lettering—vertiginous, slightly cramped, the *O*s mounted on two tiny dots—can be seen all over the world, as can the Mackintosh Rose, his orthogonal interpretation of a rose in bloom. His wife was his frequent collaborator, though as was to be the case with another famous design couple, **Charles and Ray Eames**, he tends to get most of the acclaim. In commissions such as the Willow Tearooms, which still stand in Sauchiehall Street in Glasgow, her more florid style mixes with his rectilinear geometry to great effect.

The Hill House chair is one of Mackintosh's hallmark designs. Tall, thin, and black, it has a narrow, fan-shaped seat and a laddered back that's topped with a wooden grid. Its reductive purity and graphic starkness mean that it's as much a piece of sculpture as a functional piece of furniture. The chair was intended to be used in a barrel-vaulted, creamy-white bedroom in Hill House, which Mackintosh built for the publisher Walter Blackie in Helensburgh, Scotland, in 1904. In that setting, where the only other colors are the pale green and pink flowers stenciled on the walls, it provides a measure of masculine sobriety, an effect that Mackintosh, who thought of interiors as complete works of art, would certainly have planned.

Though interest in Mackintosh's work has exploded since the art nouveau revival of the 1960s and his Glasgow School of Art is often cited as one of the finest buildings in Britain, few of his designs were built in his lifetime. Frustrated and broke, he gave up architecture and design for good in the early 1920s.

E.1027 TABLE (1927),
EILEEN GRAY (1878-1976)

With its curved chrome outlines and adjustable glass top, the E.1027 side table seems specially designed to hold a flotilla of Jazz Age cocktail implements. In 1927, the year it was created, it was as modern as a **Chanel** frock or a **surrealist** painting. Like all that was new in design in the 1920s, it firmly turned its back on the past. But the E.1027, despite its *Metropolis*-sounding name and revolutionary form, wasn't designed by some bright young thing. Eileen Gray was well into her forties when she created it, and she'd made her name first as a designer of Japanese-inspired lacquered screens and geometric rugs, not chrome-and-glass furniture.

Gray was something of an autodidact. Born into an aristocratic family in Ireland, she attended the Slade School of Art in London but never formally studied design or architecture. It was her friend Jean Badovici, a Romanian architect and journalist, who encouraged her to try her hand at architecture by building a house for him in the south of France. They named it E.1027, a code that represented their initials. *E* was for Eileen; 10 was for *J,* the tenth letter of the alphabet; 2 was for *B;* and 7 was for *G.* Built into the side of a cliff, with floor-to-ceiling windows that let in the sun and the sound of the

Eileen Gray's
E.1027 side table

sea and with a balcony that was accessible from every room, E.1027 was designed to be completely open to its surroundings. The spare, minimal interior was complemented by Gray's pared-down furniture, including the famous E.1027 table. In keeping with the free-flowing nature of the house, she designed it to be light, movable, and adaptable—its semicircular base means that it can be slid under a bed or sofa, and its lockable telescopic leg (which is topped with a handle for maximum ease of use) allows the tabletop to be adjusted to various heights. Though she was an admirer of **Le Corbusier**'s, the leading modern architect of the time, Gray disagreed with his idea that "the house is a machine to live in." Her approach to design was more humanist. "Formulas are nothing," she said. "Life is everything."

Badovici lived in the house until his death in 1956, after which it fell into disrepair. Gray seemed destined to be a footnote to design history until a 1968 magazine article prompted renewed interest in her work from collectors such as **Yves Saint Laurent**.

WASSILY CHAIR (1925),
MARCEL BREUER (1902–1981)

Marcel Breuer studied and worked at the Bauhaus, the hugely influential German art and architecture school of the 1920s and '30s known for its simple, geometric designs. Its founder, the seminal modernist architect Walter Gropius (1883–1969), believed that art, craft, and technology should be used in tandem

Marcel Breuer's Wassily chair

to create good design, a tenet that became one of the cornerstones of Bauhaus teaching. The Hungarian-born Breuer was first a precocious student and then the head of the cabinetmaker's shop at the school.

From 1919, the year it was founded, to 1925, the Bauhaus was located in Weimar. In 1925, the political climate in Germany prompted the school to move to Dessau, a larger industrial center. Here, the school's relationship with technology changed from a theoretical one to a practical

one. With state-of-the-art factories on its doorstep, the output of the Bauhaus became far more industrial. In Weimar, Breuer had worked with wood and textiles woven on the school's looms; in Dessau, he began experimenting with steel tubes.

The idea for the Wassily chair, named for the Russian abstract painter Wassily Kandinsky (1866–1944), a friend and fellow Bauhaus instructor, apparently came to Breuer as he was glancing down at his handlebars while riding his bicycle. He had his design produced outside of the school workshops, possibly because they couldn't handle the heating and bending of the steel tubes, and hired a plumber to weld together the tubes for the prototype.

Though the original had four legs, Breuer's final design is far more cunning. Steel tubes loop to form two runners, then curve up and across to form a frame from which the canvas seat, itself stretched across a U-shaped tube, is slung. The armrests are stretched across the top of this frame, and the two-piece backrest is stretched across a second U shape that's welded to the one that forms the seat. All the elements are mutually stabilizing. It looks like a series of rubber bands bridging a collection of paper clips, but it's actually quite comfortable. And like a high-end version of IKEA furniture, the Wassily armchair was designed to be easily assembled and disassembled and packs flat.

In 1933, the Nazis shut down the Bauhaus and production on the chair was halted. The school reopened briefly in Chicago in 1937, but the Wassily wasn't manufactured again until the late 1960s, when the Italian manufacturer Cassina stepped in to meet the demand for modernist classics. Breuer, meanwhile, immigrated to the United States, where he became a well-known architect, building, among other things, the Whitney Museum of American Art in New York.

CHAISE LONGUE LC4 (1928),
LE CORBUSIER (1887-1965)

Few chairs are as elegant as Le Corbusier's sleek recliner. Built of tubular steel and leather, it's a slimmed-down version of the nineteenth-century fainting couch; you can imagine a shingled Mme Recamier lounging on it.

Primarily an architect, the Swiss-born Le Corbusier (his real name was Charles-Edouard Jeanneret; he adopted his important-sounding handle in 1920) was one of the foremost practitioners of what came to be known as the international style, the dominant form of architecture in the 1920s and '30s. He wrote extensively about the theoretical aspects of design and advocated a particularly rigorous form of modernism that rejected any form of ornamentation; he supposedly once said that by law, all buildings should be white. An influential urban planner, he intended his architecture to provide an alternative to the overcrowding of inner cities—his series of Unité d'Habitation housing developments in Europe,

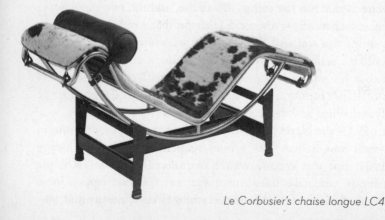

Le Corbusier's chaise longue LC4

probably his most famous buildings, address this concern—but his critics found his work dehumanizing and unfriendly.

In his private commissions, Le Corbusier was similarly stark. His geometric concrete houses, such as the Villa Savoye, feature wide-open spaces and plate-glass windows unsoftened by anything as bourgeois as drapes. Similarly, the furniture he created for them was intended to complement their uncompromisingly modern interiors. Against the abstract painting–adorned white walls of a Le Corbusier villa, the LC4, which was described in the catalog for the Salon d'Automne in 1929 as the "interior equipment of a dwelling," would look right at home.

> **PRONUNCIATION GUIDE**
>
> **Le Corbusier:**
> **LUH kor-BOO-zee-ay**

The LC4 was one of Le Corbusier's first forays into furniture design, and was a collaboration with two other architects, his cousin Pierre Jeanneret and Charlotte Perriand. They intended the LC4 to be mass-produced, but it proved to be much too expensive to manufacture, and only a limited quantity was made. The chair consists of a leather or pony-skin (very much in vogue at the time it was designed) cover stretched over an angled, tubular steel frame, which in turn rests on an H-shaped tubular steel base. In an early example of ergonomic design, it has an adjustable seat cushion and a bolster-shaped headrest.

Though the amount of furniture Le Corbusier created was tiny compared to his architectural output, he was the quintessential modernist designer, and his influence can be seen in the work of everyone from **Arne Jacobsen** to **Philippe Starck**. The LC4 is still manufactured today, by the Italian company Cassina.

SAVOY VASE (1936), ALVAR AALTO (1898–1976)

With only its organic curves to give it decorative interest, the otherwise perfectly plain Savoy vase gave the design world a surprise when it was first produced in 1936. One of the earliest examples of abstract form in glassware, it was the winning entry in the Finnish glass manufacturer Karhula-Iittala's competition to find new tableware and art-glass designs for the World Exposition in Paris in 1937, and went on to be a touchstone of midcentury style. With its tapering sides and tactile curves, the Savoy vase is a pleasing object in itself. But it's when it's filled with flowers that its possibilities are revealed. Unlike most vases, which allow for only one place to arrange stems, the Savoy's wavelike sides mean that individual combinations are possible.

The vase's blend of abstraction and natural motifs is characteristic of the Finnish architect, town planner, and furniture, lighting, and glassware designer Alvar Aalto's work. Its fluid outline was apparently inspired by the shorelines of Finland's many lakes—a particularly neat analogy, given that the vase was intended to be filled with water—although critics also point to Aalto's familiarity with **surrealist** artists such as Jean Arp and his interest in Japanese woodcuts as possible influences. Whatever his inspiration, the Savoy vase was to have a huge impact on Aalto's career: Its undulating form was in turn the stimulus for his Finnish Pavilion at the New York World's Fair of 1939, a building that brought him enormous international acclaim.

The vase—actually a series of vases, ranging in size from three inches to thirty-nine inches tall—ran into production problems almost immediately after winning first prize. Aalto wanted to create the mold from sheets of metal threaded through steel rods to give the desired curves, a technique that would have made remodeling possible. When this proved impractical, wood molds were used.

Alvar Aalto's Savoy vases

Aalto initially gave his design the **dada**-esque title Eskimo Girl's Leather Breeches, but the name didn't stick. The vase is usually known as the Savoy in honor of the Savoy restaurant in Helsinki, which had earlier commissioned Aalto and his wife, the architect Aino Marsio, to design its interiors and then bought the vases as well.

Though the Savoy vase was Aalto's most popular glassware design and is still in production, the designer never made a dime from its sales. Because the design belonged to the factory that sponsored the competition, all Aalto ever got for his iconic vase was the prize money.

AMERICAN MODERN TABLE SERVICE (1937), RUSSEL WRIGHT (1905–1976)

Fifty years before Martha Stewart prompted Americans to remake themselves in her image, Russel Wright was prodding them toward a more stylish life. He didn't have Martha's media empire to help him, but between his designs and the decorating and entertaining guides he wrote with his wife, Mary, Wright shaped the look and feel of mid-century American homes.

Tactile and earthy, American Modern didn't look like anything else then available. The pieces were curvy and tapered, with big,

Russel Wright's American modern dinner service

loop-shaped handles on the pitchers and teapots. And the glossy, mottled colors—chartreuse curry, bean brown, black chutney—were a radical departure from the flowers-on-a-white-background cliché of traditional china. In keeping with Wright's philosophy that home entertaining should be relaxed and informal, pleasurable for host and guest alike, American Modern was both sophisticated enough to feel special and folksy enough for everyday use.

Wright wasn't the first to push consumers toward modern design, but he was the first to do so in a price range that appealed to the middle class. Wright was, says the social historian and critic Russell Lynes, "the answer for those of us brought up to accept the Bauhaus doctrine as announcing the design wave of the present and hope of the future, but who could not afford to buy the expensive imports of **Le Corbusier** and **Mies van der Rohe** and **Marcel Breuer**. . . . Ours was, I assure you, no small clique. We were part of the mass market for which Wright designed and proud of it."

It took Wright two years to find a manufacturer willing to produce his designs, but his persistence paid off: American Modern went on to sell more than eighty million pieces between 1939 and 1959. Wright encouraged sales by giving customers the option to build their dinner services piece by piece, from open stock, rather than committing to an entire set at once. The design was so popular that in the mid-1950s, the Ideal Toy Company made miniature plastic replicas for children to play with.

Wright's range was enormous. Along with dinner services, he went on to create table linens, furniture, accessories, glassware, and art pottery, all of it in keeping with the ethos that he expressed in the title of one of his books: *Good Design Is for Everyone*. Today, enough people still believe in that ethos to make anything Russel Wright made a collector's item. As **Andy Warhol**, who owned an enormous collection of his work, said, "Who's good after him?"

ANT CHAIR (1952),
ARNE JACOBSEN (1902–1971)

Even if you're not familiar with any of the other objects described in this section, you've seen, and more than likely sat on, the Ant chair. Since Arne Jacobsen designed it in 1952, the Ant has been used in countless kitchens, dining rooms, offices, and restaurants. Unpretentious, cheerful, and versatile, it's an example of modern design that comes free of any overly intellectualized preciousness. But then, unlike the modern furniture of the 1920s and '30s, which tends toward the sterile, postwar designs often had more organic, fluid lines. They're easier to love than **Le Corbusier**'s rather formidable chaise longue.

Jacobsen created the 3100, as the Ant was officially known, for the canteen of the Danish pharmaceutical company Novo Nordisk, which wanted a chair that was stable, portable, and easy to stack. The familiar nickname came about because looked at straight on, the chair's curvy plywood body resembles an ant with its head raised. The back and seat

Arne Jacobsen's
Ant chair

are made of one sheet of molded wood, pinched in at the middle, where the small of the back rests. This is attached to tubular steel legs. Jacobsen designed the Ant with three legs, and though you can now buy a four-legged version and even a swiveling office version, he resisted attempts to tinker with his beloved original, and other versions weren't produced until after his death. Though Novo Nordisk ordered only thirty of Jacobsen's chairs, he designed them to be mass produced, and their manufacturer, Fritz Hansen, tested two hundred prototypes before going ahead with production. They've since made and sold more than five million Ants.

The Ant proved so successful that between 1952 and 1961 Jacobsen designed a series of variations, the most famous being the 3107, more familiarly known as the Seven. This is the chair Christine Keeler, the call girl who brought down a British government, is straddling in Lewis Morley's famous 1963 photo of her. The photo was taken to promote a film Keeler was in, and which she'd agreed to do nude publicity shots for. But when the time came to take the photos, Keeler balked. Morley persuaded her to sit astride the Seven

chair, which, while she was technically naked, covered her. The shot
is one of the decade's defining images and made the chair almost as
famous as Keeler was at the time. But much to Jacobsen's dismay,
that particular chair was merely a copy of his design.

LOUNGE CHAIR AND OTTOMAN (1956), CHARLES (1907-1978) AND RAY KAISER (1912-1988) EAMES

Few people had more influence on American design in the twentieth century than Charles Eames and Ray Kaiser Eames. They first
collaborated in 1940; by the time they were married a year later,
their ideas were so entwined that everything that was produced by
them from that date onward, including buildings, furniture, and
interiors and exhibition designs, is considered a joint effort. Their
bentwood lounge chair and ottoman, made by gluing together and
laminating layers of rosewood, is one of their most iconic creations
and is often referred to simply as an Eames chair. Both conceptual
and homey, it exemplifies the Eameses' down-to-earth approach to
design.

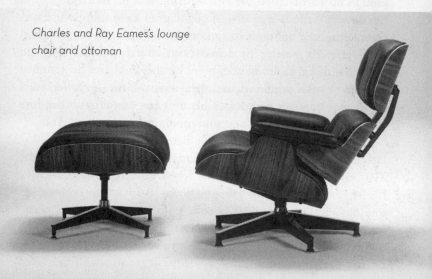

*Charles and Ray Eames's lounge
chair and ottoman*

Charles had experimented with molding wood in the late 1930s, when he collaborated with **Eero Saarinen**. The pair entered the Organic Design competition held by the Museum of Modern Art in New York in 1940, and their bentwood designs, though never produced on a large scale, won first prize in two categories. Charles and Ray continued to produce bent-wood furniture in their California studio throughout the '40s and '50s. The 1956 chair and ottoman, originally conceived of as a present for their friend the film director Billy Wilder, is the most expensive and most comfortable (Charles said he wanted it to have "the warm, receptive look of a well-used first-baseman's mitt") of these designs. The chair is made of three doubly curved rosewood shells—headrest, back, and seat—padded with leather-covered rubber; the accompanying ottoman is made of a fourth doubly curved shell. Each part of the chair is completely adjustable, and both the chair and the ottoman are mounted on pivoting star bases. This sounds complicated, but it isn't: The chair was designed to be assembled or taken apart by one person armed with nothing but a screwdriver. The Eameses even made a short film—filmmaking was another outlet for their seemingly boundless creativity—demonstrating this.

The Eameses were pioneers in using innovative techniques in the service of practical design. Along with bent plywood, they experimented with fiberglass and plastic resin. The house they designed for themselves in 1947, one of a series of Case Study Houses for *Arts & Architecture* magazine, was hugely influential in its use of prefabricated parts. Yet while they didn't shy away from embracing the new, their designs were never completely unfamiliar. Their own house, for example, was filled with the toys and cultural artifacts they collected.

The Eameses' studio remained open until Ray's death, ten years to the day after her husband died. The Herman Miller furniture company continues to manufacture their designs.

THE APPLE MACINTOSH (1984),
HARTMUT ESSLINGER (B. 1944) AND FROG DESIGN

If you are a Mac user, you know one thing for certain: Macs are cooler than PCs. It's a truism that's best illustrated by the perceived schism that divides the two: PCs are for the serious business of work; Macs are for play. But it wasn't always this way. Prior to 1984, computers, whether made by IBM, Apple, or anyone else, were pretty dull. The market was aimed at the specialist, not the layman, and no one ever got excited about what the things looked like. But all that changed in January of that year, when Apple released the first-ever Macintosh, soon nicknamed the Mac.

The Mac was Apple's eureka moment. It took a piece of mundane office equipment and made it sexy. In technical terms, the Mac was the first commercially successful personal computer to employ a graphical user interface (GUI) and a mouse rather than the then standard command-line interface. This was a huge step in demystifying computing; instead of typing in strings of commands, you pointed and clicked. Moreover, from an aesthetic point of view, the Macintosh was light-years ahead of the competition. The squat little box looked designed, while everything else appeared to be merely assembled.

The Apple Macintosh SE, designed by Harmut Esslinger and Frog Design

In visually setting the Mac apart from every other computer on the market, Hartmut Esslinger and his team at Frog Design made it an object of desire, a design philosophy that Apple embraces to this day (and backs up with leading-edge technology). First was its color, a creamy white that was instantly identifiable in the sea of dingy beigeness that was IBM and its clones. Then there was the monitor-keyboard-mouse setup, now the industry standard. By breaking the Mac down into three components, they put it within the grasp of the computer illiterate. You looked at the screen, you typed with the keyboard, and you navigated with the mouse. Easy.

What cemented the Mac's rebellious image was the commercial that introduced it. Directed by Ridley Scott and created by the advertising agency Chiat/Day, it showed an unnamed heroine running into a hall packed with workers watching Big Brother (i.e., IBM) on a giant screen. She hurls the sledgehammer she's carrying at the image, destroying it. The voice-over concludes: "On January 24, Apple Computer will introduce Macintosh. And you'll see why 1984 won't be like *1984*."

THE JUICY SALIF (1990), PHILIPPE STARCK (B. 1949)

When you look at everything Philippe Starck's designed in the past thirty years—an output that ranges from Alessi kitchen gadgets to Target tape dispensers, the Vittel mineral-water bottle to the Excalibur toilet brush, Paris nightclubs to New York hotels—you can't help but wonder if it isn't Philippe Starck's world, and we're just living in it. By far the most prolific designer of his generation, Starck is an international superstar, and his designs, by turns campy, glamorous, referential, and sarcastic, are a barometer of the age. As are his life and working styles: The peripatetic Starck divides his time between Paris, New York, London, and Buraro, Italy, and thinks of himself as "a Japanese architect, an American art director, a German industrial designer, a French artistic director, an Italian furniture designer." Of his working style, he says, "I work instinctively, and above all fast. I can design a good piece of furniture in fifteen minutes."

Philippe Starck's Juicy Salif juicer

His career began in the late '60s in his hometown of Paris, where he designed inflatable houses. He then went to work as an art director at Pierre Cardin. In the 1970s, he created the interiors for two of the city's seminal nightclubs, La Main Bleue and Les Bains-Douches. He adroitly balanced the bad-boy reputation those commissions gave him by designing the furnishings for François Mitterrand's living quarters in the Palais Elysée in 1982, the job that gave him a presence on the world stage and made him one of the foremost furniture designers of the decade.

To those who like design to be practical and neat, the Juicy Salif presents complications. A cast-aluminum lemon squeezer that looks like an alien spacecraft on stilts, it streamlines the juicing process by eliminating the sieve that catches the pits and pulp and by having the juice flow directly into the glass. If you think that a juicer should prevent the pits and pulp from landing in the juice, this is problematic. On the other hand, if you think of design as primarily aesthetic, then the Juicy Salif's beauty and simplicity, not to mention the stylish thrill it lends to an otherwise mundane task, outweigh its drawbacks.

FIVE AFFORDABLE DESIGN OBJECTS TO OWN

GOOD DESIGN DOESN'T EXIST just to be photographed in decorating magazines—it's meant to be enjoyed. The following are five ways to show off your good taste while simultaneously adding pleasure to your life.

ANGLEPOISE LAMP (1934), GEORGE CARWARDINE (1887-1948)

No life is complete without a desk—where else are you going to do your thinking?—and no desk is complete without a good desk lamp. The granddaddy of superior desk lamps is the Anglepoise, which was first produced in 1934. Its creator was a British automotive engineer named George Carwardine, who based his design on a new type of spring he'd invented that could remain in position even after being moved in every possible direction. Though lighting was a secondary interest for him (springs were his real passion), Carwardine soon realized the potential of a light source that could be so precisely focused. Inspired by the constant-tension principle of the human arm, he designed a lamp that was both flexible and, thanks to its heavy base, stable. His design, with a few updates, is still in production today. It's been imitated by everyone from IKEA on up, but nothing compares to the real thing.

TIMOR PERPETUAL DESK CALENDAR (1967), ENZO MARI (B. 1932)

If your approach to buying a calendar is at all typical, it probably consists of trying to find the least-offensive kitty imagery possible in the January sales. But converting to the Timor perpetual calendar means more than never having to buy another example of schlocky cat photography—the sleek white or black plastic stand, with its adjustable date, day, and month arms, is a piece of interactive modernist sculpture that will make any desk look instantly better. As the days and months roll along, the various arms pivot back into the stand, and their successors are pulled out to replace them. The Timor was created in 1967 by the almost-too-thoughtful-for-his-own-good Italian designer Enzo Mari (he once spent a year devising the perfect ashtray, only to have it rejected by customers), who based the calendar's arms on the train signals he remembered seeing as a child.

MOLESKINE NOTEBOOK (1998)

Important life lesson: Always carry a notebook (and something to write with, naturally). You can't do better than a Moleskine, the lightweight black notebook with the expandable back pocket (perfect for storing business cards and receipts), sewn spine (which allows it to lie flat when open), and

PRONUNCIATION GUIDE

**Moleskine:
moh-luh-SKEE-na**

elastic band (which either holds the book shut or acts as a page marker). Available in different sizes and with a choice of blank or ruled pages and a hard or soft cover, it's the sort of chic but functional *cahier* you can imagine jotting fashion show notes into—or using to record your impressions of a trek up Everest. Modo & Modo, who began producing Moleskines after the original publisher went out of business, claims that these notebooks were used by **Picasso** and Hemingway, but the latest incarnation isn't a direct descendant of the original. Just as good an endorsement is the fact that this is the only notepad in existence with blogs and fan sites devoted to it.

THE SELF SHELF (2002),
NICOLE VAN SCHOUWENBURG (B. 1958)

As noted in Ten Books You Should Read, literature is the foundation of the well-furnished mind. But where is its place in the well-furnished apartment? Floor-to-ceiling shelves are the ideal, but if you haven't quite got those together yet, consider the Self shelf, the shelf that looks like a book. Mount it to the wall, pile on up to eight and a half pounds of Proust (or something less weighty), and—ta-da—your stack will appear to be floating against the wall. The trick behind the Dutch duo of Nicole van Schouwenburg and Irene Klinkenberg's trompe-l'oeil bluff is their witty realism and hidden hardware. It comes in three different sizes (novel, pocket, and cookbook) and five different cover designs, including *Ceci n'est pas un livre* (a play on **surrealist** René Magritte's famous pipe painting), which looks like an old art book, and the vintage crime-thriller-style *The Mystery of the Floating Piles*.

WASHING-UP BOWL AND BRUSH (2002),
OLE JENSEN (B. 1958) FOR NORMANN
COPENHAGEN

Nothing banishes the delusions of glamour brought on by a successful dinner party with quite the same point-blank efficiency as washing the dishes afterward. But while those rubber gloves with the faux red manicure and plastic cocktail ring your grandmother gave you are too kitsch even to have any redeeming camp value, Danish designer Ole Jensen's pleasantly squishy basin and accompanying wooden scrub brush actually make the whole dreary task of scraping, soaping, and rinsing feel somewhat stylish, and that's no mean feat. The award-winning Jensen, whose design philosophy revolves around heightening the enjoyment of everyday tasks, has devised a flexible basin, made of durable rubber in six different colors, which adds an element of fun to an otherwise mindless chore. And the contrasting angled brush, with its hand-fixed natural bristles, is vaguely retro. Together they may not lead to a love of housework, but they're certainly natty.

| **PRONUNCIATION GUIDE** |
| Ole Jensen: |
| ooh-LAY YEN-sen |

TEN LANDMARK BUILDINGS AND THEIR ARCHITECTS

IF YOU'VE EVER HAD THE LUCK to walk into the old TWA Terminal at JFK (sadly, it's now closed), you know the power that good architecture has. With its soaring, atomic-age curves and sinuous lines, the terminal suggests all the glamour and color and potential of travel—which is not the feeling you usually get from airports. All the following buildings inspire that same sense of wonder.

CASA BATLLÓ (1907), ANTONI GAUDÍ (1852-1926)

With its asymmetrically curved roof, mottled façade of blue, green, and purple broken ceramic tiles, and lacy balconies, Casa Batlló looks like a storybook castle drawn by an artistically precocious child. Remodeled from an existing—and far more pedestrian—building

PRONUNCIATION GUIDE
Casa Batlló: CA-za bat-YO

in 1907 for the wealthy textile magnate Joseph Batlló, it's one of the Catalonian architect Antoni Gaudí's most spectacular works.

Gaudí was the leading architect of *moderisme*, Catalonia's home-grown version of **art nouveau**, and Barcelona, the city where he spent his career and with which he is indelibly linked, is dotted with his biomorphic, whipped-cream fantasies. Sagrada Familia, a still-unfinished basilica that looks like it's been carved from melted wax, is probably the most famous, but few can match Casa Batlló for sheer exuberance.

> **PRONUNCIATION GUIDE**
>
> **Antoni Gaudí:**
> **ann-TOE-nee gow-DEE**

Thanks to Gaudí's vivid imagination and talent for integrating architectural styles—Moorish, neo-Gothic—into his work, the building is especially inventive in its ability to suggest other forms. Viewed from a distance, it looks like a sleeping dragon curled up on Barcelona's stately Passeig de Gràcia. The skeletal-looking posts and grillwork of the balconies, meanwhile, have prompted locals to nickname it the House of Bones. The free-form windows resemble leaves, while the dappled ceramics that cover the outside suggest Monet's water lilies. Inside, hallways look like underwater grottoes and the irregularly shaped walls seem to waver like the sea.

Like all Gaudí's buildings, Casa Batlló is rooted in nature. When he was a child, illness kept him from playing with his siblings and friends, and he spent hours studying and drawing in the countryside near his parents' home. When he became an architect, he rejected the geometry of straight lines and right angles, preferring to translate the helicoids, hyperbolas, and parabolas he observed in the natural world into the vaults and arches that give his buildings their characteristic airiness and spaciousness.

An intensely religious man, Gaudí retreated from secular life in his later years and worked exclusively on Sagrada Familia, regarding it as his crowning achievement. After his patron died in 1916, he was virtually penniless, but carried on with his work. In 1926, he was hit by a tram while crossing the street and taken to a public hospital. When his friends found him the next day, he refused to move, saying he belonged with the poor. He died two days later and was buried in the crypt of Sagrada Familia.

FALLINGWATER (1937),
FRANK LLOYD WRIGHT (1867–1959)

How important was Frank Lloyd Wright? To say that contemporary architecture wouldn't be the same without him isn't an exaggeration. His open floor plans, incorporation of natural elements and local materials, and his insistence that a building relate to its surroundings, once novel, are now givens. As Simon and Garfunkel sang of him— and not many architects are immortalized in pop songs—"Architects may come and architects may go / And never change your point of view / When I run dry I stop awhile and think of you."

Fallingwater kicked off the second, most prolific phase of Wright's career. As a young architect in Illinois at the turn of the twentieth century, he had become known for his Prairie Houses. But he hadn't designed any larger structures, and by the 1930s, upstarts like **Le Corbusier** and **Mies van der Rohe** were being lauded for their avant-garde buildings. Wright, who was then almost seventy, appeared to be at the end of his career.

That changed in 1934, when Edgar and Liliane Kaufmann asked Wright to design a weekend house for them in Bear Run, Pennsylvania. Despite the fact that he hadn't received a commission in years, Wright didn't exactly spring into action. He and the Kaufmanns visited the site in late 1934, but it wasn't until September of 1935 that he produced the plans for Fallingwater. According to Wright lore, he drew them up in the two hours it took Edgar Kaufmann to drive from Milwaukee to Wright's house in Spring Green, Wisconsin, one Sunday morning.

As its name suggests, Fallingwater stands by a waterfall. But instead of giving it the expected view of the waterfall, Wright placed it above the falls, so that the only experience of the waterfall from inside the house is the sound of water rushing over rocks. His setting was inspired: Seen from below the falls, as it was in a famous *Time* magazine cover, the house's cantilevered terraces seem to float above the river. The modernity of these thick concrete slabs is contrasted with the sandstone pillars the house stands on and interior details such as the boulder that serves as the hearth for the living-room fireplace. With all these elements working in harmony,

Fallingwater is both a brilliant example of organic, site-specific architecture and a modernist triumph.

Though Wright's design wasn't especially sound (he was always more of a visionary than an engineer) and Fallingwater has needed shoring up over the years, it's still regarded as the most influential house of the twentieth century and was instrumental in getting Wright the kind of splashy commissions he craved, including the one for the Solomon R. Guggenheim Museum in New York.

LOVELL HEALTH HOUSE (1929), RICHARD NEUTRA (1892–1970)

Perhaps because he was strictly a domestic architect, with no big-name projects attached to his name, interest in Richard Neutra faded away as his career wound down. But in the past dozen years, both his reputation and his modernist California aesthetic have rebounded spectacularly, with his houses used as backdrops for fashion shoots and advertising campaigns. And in 1997, Neutra's crowning achievement, the Lovell Health House, was featured in the film *L.A. Confidential*, where its immaculate white terraces, perched high above the city below, are a visual metaphor for sleek West Coast living at its most stylish.

The Austrian-born Neutra studied with the architectural visionary Adolph Loos in Vienna in the period just before the First World War, when the city was a cultural boomtown. Neutra soaked up the stimuli, but his idol was **Frank Lloyd Wright**, and in 1923 he made his way to the U.S. to work with him. From there he journeyed on to Los Angeles, where he and his wife, Dione, joined his university friend Rudolf Schindler, also an architect, and his wife, Pauline. The couples lived communally for five years, and the two men were briefly business partners. But though both went on to be major talents, they never built anything together, and eventually stopped speaking—a split that was a direct result of Neutra's winning the commission for the Lovell Health House. The client, a naturopath named

---

PRONUNCIATION GUIDE

**Richard Neutra:
RI-chard NOY-tra**

Philip Lovell, had previously commissioned several vacation houses from Schindler but chose to go with Neutra for his city dwelling. Neutra denied lobbying for the appointment, but Schindler never forgave his friend for snagging the job he considered rightfully his.

The Lovell House was the first all-steel-frame house ever built in the U.S., and Neutra was so nervous about the project that he acted as his own contractor. He and his crew erected the multistoried frame in sections, then transported it to the steep hillside location. Once the entire structure was up, they covered it with sprayed concrete to form the walls. Most photos of the house show only the main body of the building, where its cascade of balconies—which are suspended from the roof frame with thin steel cables rather than cantilevered, a construction technique that caused a stir at the time—stack up like thick pieces of chalk. But the house is best seen as an L-shaped whole, with Neutra's tiered landscaping filling in the open space.

Lovell was ecstatic about the house—perhaps because it was Neutra's habit to have his clients fill out detailed questionnaires to determine exactly how they wanted to live—which couldn't have made Schindler very happy. Hailed as a masterwork, the Lovell House propelled Neutra into architecture's front ranks. It's now on L.A.'s register of historic places.

SEAGRAM BUILDING (1958), LUDWIG MIES VAN DER ROHE (1886–1969)

Ludwig Mies van der Rohe had one overarching, lifelong ambition: to create an architectural style that embodied the modern era, the way Gothic cathedrals embodied the Middle Ages or classical temples embodied ancient Greece. In what can be read as an ironic twist, he got his wish, in the glass box that is the modern office building. The Seagram Building, a bronze glass box that stands in midtown Manhattan, is a paragon of this omnipresent form of twentieth-century architecture.

Like many leading modernists, Mies (he was born Maria Ludwig Michael Mies, the son of a stonecutter, but

PRONUNCIATION GUIDE

**Mies van der Rohe:
MEEZ van der ROW**

adopted the aristocratic-sounding van der Rohe as a young man) was associated with the Bauhaus. He taught there in its final years and served as its last director. During this period he designed some of the century's most iconic pieces of modern furniture, most notably the Barcelona chair, a sort of steel-and-leather camp chair that's become a mainstay of waiting rooms and reception areas. But his work was judged "un-German" by the Nazis, and in 1937 Mies emigrated to America.

He settled in Chicago, where he took on commissions such as 860–880 Lakeshore Drive, twin glass-and-steel apartment towers, and the Farnsworth House, a stark, startling modern pavilion/country house set down in sixty acres of woods. By the time the Canadian distiller Seagram approached him to design its New York headquarters, Mies was one of the most highly regarded architects in the world.

The Seagram Building is the pinnacle of the International Style, which held that a building's structural elements should be visible from the outside. Like most large buildings of the time, the Seagram Building was built on a steel frame from which nonstructural glass walls were hung. Mies wanted to make this frame visible, but was prevented from doing so because building codes required that structural steel be covered with fireproofing to prevent it from melting in a blaze. Determined to get his "skin and bone" structure, Mies faked it by using nonstructural bronze-toned I beams to get the look he desired. So while the Seagram Building looks like it's letting it all hang out, it's really not.

Mies's collaborator on the project was the American architect (and Mies fan) Philip Johnson, who designed the building's Four Seasons restaurant. The **abstract expressionist** Mark Rothko painted the restaurant's murals, with the avowed intention to "ruin the appetite of every son of a bitch who ever eats in that room." Despite his best efforts, it didn't work—the Four Seasons is still one of New York's preeminent power-lunch destinations.

TWA AIRPORT TERMINAL (1962),
EERO SAARINEN (1910-1961)

Though it's becoming increasingly difficult to imagine, there was a time, back in the early days of the commercial jetliner, when air travel was considered glamorous, exotic—even fun. Catching a flight was a reason to dress up (if this sounds too far-fetched to be true, rent the 1963 film *The V.I.P.s,* a Liz Taylor–Richard Burton extravaganza about the nascent jet set for proof).

> **PRONUNCIATION GUIDE**
>
> **Eero Saarinen:**
> **EAR-oh SAHR-i-nen**

No building embodies the thrill and dynamism of travel more stylishly than Finnish-born Eero Saarinen's Trans World Airlines Terminal at John F. Kennedy International Airport in New York (though it's been closed since 2001, it has been declared a designated landmark). It even looks like it's moving: The two outstretched concrete wings of its roof give it the appearance of a bird in mid-flight.

In choosing Saarinen to design its flagship terminal, TWA made an inspired choice. Though he was only just beginning to come out of the shadow of his father, the prominent architect Eliel Saarinen—the two had just collaborated on a Mies-influenced corporate campus for General Motors—the younger Saarinen had already stated that he had "an urge to soar." His plans for the Gateway Arch over St. Louis, Missouri (designed in 1948, it wasn't completed until after Saarinen's death), and his curvaceous Tulip chair (1956) both show his love of swooping lines.

Though the powerful thrust of the TWA Terminal's roof is inspiring, it's the interior of the building where Saarinen's concept really takes off. It's designed as a metaphor for the experience of flight. The arching ceiling represents the sky; the narrow bridge that bisects its spaciousness is the symbolic horizon. Everything, even the vaguely cloud-shaped departures board, contributes to the illusion that gravity is loosening its grip, a sensation that's magnified by the rounded tunnels that are used to get out onto the tarmac. They incline gently upward, as though they were lifting you to the imminent takeoff.

Though all this was a hit with airline passengers, critics were initially inclined to be harsh. They took exception to Saarinen's design process: Rather than analyzing the terminal's uses and functions and devising a building that expressed these in an elegant way, he had begun with an image, then figured out how to make it work. Eventually, however, most naysayers admitted that the building was not without its merits. But Saarinen never saw his design come to fruition—he died of a brain tumor the year before the terminal was completed.

CENTRE GEORGES POMPIDOU (1977), RENZO PIANO (B. 1937) AND RICHARD ROGERS (B. 1933)

With its colorful exoskeleton of pipes and ducts, the Centre Georges Pompidou rises up out of the narrow medieval streets of Paris's Beaubourg neighborhood like a colossal Rubik's cube. It's a building you immediately love or hate. To those in the former camp, the building's inside-out construction is exuberant and playful. Those who can't stand it think the architects' decision to put all the service structures on the outside and color-code their coverings—blue for air-conditioning, green for water, yellow for electricity, red for the escalators, and white for the ventilation shafts—is just plain ugly. (The steel beams that hold the building up are also on the outside, but they're just metal colored.) Either way you look at it, Pompidou, or Beaubourg, as it's known, is as much a Paris landmark as the Eiffel Tower.

The building was the result of a design competition launched in 1971 by then French president Georges Pompidou. The idea was to create a new cultural center, but the winning design, submitted by Renzo Piano of Italy and Richard Rogers of the U.K., was far less imposing than your average marble museum. Their win was controversial, the more so when it emerged that they were young, unknown, and not French. Both Piano and Rogers have since gone on to have exemplary careers; both have won architecture's highest honor, the Pritzker Prize, and Rogers is currently designing one of the new office towers at the former World Trade Center site (Rogers's career did have a rather high-profile low point, however—he was one of the most vocal advocates of London's Millennium Dome, a politically controversial structure by the Thames that many Londoners loathe).

But in 1971, they were upstarts, building what came to be seen as a symbol of the high-tech school of architecture. Their design was inspired by a structure that was never built: Cedric Price's Fun Palace, which was conceived of in 1964 as a flexible, temporary frame-structure cultural space. Like the imagined Fun Palace, Pompidou is indeed very flexible. Because its innards have been moved to the out-side, it's wide-open inside—each of its six floors offers 80,000 square feet of column-free space. It houses a huge library, the Musée National d'Art Moderne, various design centers, a bookstore, several cafés, and the perennially crowded rooftop restaurant, Le Georges. The plaza at the front of the building, which gets crowded as soon as the temperature rises in the spring, features a fountain with sculp-tures by Niki de Saint-Phalle and Jean Tinguely.

THE LOUVRE PYRAMID (1989), I. M. PEI (B. 1917)

When it was revealed in 1981 that the Chinese American architect I. M. Pei had been commissioned to renovate the Louvre, France's most sacred cultural site, Paris's chattering classes were shocked. No one can tamper with the Louvre and come away unscathed, but be-ing a foreigner only exacerbates matters, as the Italian Gian Lorenzo Bernini learned when he was hired by Louis XIV to finish the palace in the seventeenth century. Though he was one of the most distin-guished artists of the age, Bernini was paid and summarily dismissed, his plans ignored as though he were just another hired hand. Fran-çois Mitterrand, the newly elected president of the Republic who personally selected Pei for his pet project, assured the architect that what had happened to Bernini would not happen to him.

For one who's been awarded the prestigious Pritzker Prize and is recognized as one of the foremost practitioners of modernism in the world, Pei didn't get off to an especially auspicious start. Though he trained at Harvard's Graduate School of Design under the Bauhaus luminaries Walter Gropius and **Marcel Breuer**, his first job was as the in-house architect to a real-estate developer. His reputation as an artistically sensitive architect didn't really begin until twenty years later, when Jacqueline Kennedy Onassis chose him to build the John F. Kennedy Memorial Library. This was followed by several museum commissions, most notably the East Building of the National Gallery in Washington, and, finally, the Louvre project.

Though the Louvre was undergoing a far-reaching and much-needed overhaul, what really sparked controversy was Pei's plan for the new entrance to the museum: a giant glass pyramid. Both Pei and Mitterrand, who was accused of having pharaonic delusions, were ridiculed. Today, of course, the Pyramid—it's actually two pyramids, one aboveground and the other inverted beneath it—is one of Paris's best-loved symbols. It stands 70 feet high; its square base measures 115 feet. And rather than being grandiose, it's conscious of its supporting-role status: It's made of glass, so it doesn't obstruct the view of the Renaissance masterpiece that it sets off. The Pyramid's pure lines are both an elegant contrast to the grandeur of the original building and a fittingly spectacular entrance to one of the world's greatest museums.

Every once in a while, the old canard surfaces that the Louvre Pyramid is made up of 666 planes of glass and has some sort of demonic connection (e.g., in Dan Brown's *The Da Vinci Code*). Though it's an entertaining proposition, it isn't true.

GUGGENHEIM MUSEUM BILBAO (1997), FRANK O. GEHRY (B. 1929)

For years, Pritzker Prize winner Frank O. Gehry kept his creative impulses confined to his own house, slowly customizing it with curving, organically inspired additions made of galvanized metal, plywood, and chain-link fencing. In the process, he transformed what had been a standard-issue California bungalow into a cheerfully wonky building that straddles the line between architecture and sculpture. But it wasn't until a guest asked him why he was so free at home and so staid at work that he decided to follow his impulses professionally.

That was the first step toward Gehry's developing his now-famous style, a blend of billowing amorphous shapes (he cites nature-loving **Alvar Aalto** as an influence), witty allusions to figural and metaphorical forms, and untraditional materials. In the process, he's become one of the most famous architects in the world, someone whose name is recognized almost as readily outside his profession as within.

The Guggenheim Museum in Bilbao, Spain, is Gehry's most iconic work. Because it's in a port town, it was designed to resemble a ship. But this reference shouldn't be taken too literally; the building is more abstract sculpture than anything else. It's made up of juxtaposed shapes that flow seamlessly from one into the other. Blocks of limestone, glass curtain walls, and undulating forms covered in sheets of wafer-thin titanium that changes color in the sunlight are all part of the mix. The interiors, too, are spectacular: The central atrium is crowned by a flower-shaped metal skylight that floods the soaring space with warm light; a gallery known as "the boat" stretches 427 feet in length without a single pillar.

The Guggenheim Bilbao couldn't have been built twenty years earlier—its curves are too mathematically complicated. Like all Gehry's recent work, it was constructed with the aid of modeling software known as CATIA (Computer Aided Three-dimensional Interactive Application).

The response to the Guggenheim Bilbao has been almost unanimously good, a rarity in architecture. It's been called "a miracle" *(The New York Times)* and "the most successful building of the century" *(The Observer)*. It's also given Bilbao a huge tourist boost, attracting more than a million visitors in its first year. Known as "the Guggenheim effect," this if-you-build-it-they-will-come philosophy has prompted other out-of-the-way towns (including Rioja, Spain, where Gehry recently built a hotel) to hire renowned architects to give them instant cachet.

ROSENTHAL CENTER FOR CONTEMPORARY ART (2003), ZAHA HADID (B. 1950)

It's one of architecture's acknowledged paradoxes: The most audacious and innovative thinkers often build the fewest buildings.

That's certainly been true in the case of Zaha Hadid, the Baghdad-born architect who remains the only woman to be awarded the Pritzker Prize since it was established in 1979. She's been offered big projects only to lose them, time and time again, a misfortune that's been blamed on both her flamboyant personality and her difficult-to-decipher drawings. Until the completion of the Rosenthal Center for Contemporary Art in Cincinnati, Ohio, Hadid was primarily famed for her lush paintings and meticulously detailed drawings of projects that never progressed beyond that stage, such as the Hong Kong Peak Club (a commission she won when she was only thirty-three) and the Cardiff Bay Opera House in Wales.

Hadid's influences are varied and cosmopolitan. She grew up in a Bauhaus-inspired house in Baghdad at a time when the city was one of the cosmopolitan centers of the Islamic world, and Middle Eastern intellectuals were reaching out to the West. She studied in Switzerland and Beirut and has spent time in New York, Moscow, Berlin, and London, where she studied and then worked under **Rem Koolhaas**, and where she has had her own practice since the late '70s. It's not altogether surprising, then, that one of the themes that runs throughout Hadid's work is that of a society in constant motion. Like **Eero Saarinen**, whom she's been compared to, she creates buildings of enormous dynamism.

The Rosenthal Center for Contemporary Art is a building that's best experienced by moving through it. The lobby floor curls up under the feet like an elegant half-pipe, rising to blend seamlessly into the back wall of the building. Rather than uniformly sized, distinct floors that are accessed via stairs and elevators, the rest of the building is given over to a series of ramps, stairs, and multiple box-shaped galleries that offer new vistas at every turn. These galleries can be enlarged, made smaller, or otherwise reconfigured with movable partitions. It's an ideal setting for the Center, which doesn't have a permanent collection. Instead, it sponsors a variety of changing shows (the most notorious being the 1990 retrospective of photographer Robert Mapplethorpe's work), all of which call for different exhibition spaces.

To Herbert Muschamp, the chief architecture critic for *The New York Times,* this flexibility perfectly encapsulates Hadid's work. "In the West, mobility typically holds connotations of advanced technology and displacement," he writes. "In the Middle East, it is associated

TIP SHEET

HOW TO TALK ABOUT ARCHITECTURE

You don't behave the same way in a house as you do in a monument partly due to their difference in *scale*. Buildings are constructed in relation to the human body, so that **Fallingwater**, which was built for intimate activities like sleeping and eating breakfast, is on a smaller scale than the **Louvre Pyramid**, which was meant to inspire awe and orderly queuing. *Proportion* refers to the relationship between the various parts of the building. If a building is well proportioned, even oddball configurations, like the varying window sizes of the **Casa Batlló**, look right. Some buildings—the **TWA Terminal**—take a sculptural *form*. Others—the **Centre Georges Pompidou**—are an assembly of parts. Those are two different ways of treating *space*. Architects use *color* and *texture* as a way of drawing the eye to particular features of their work. Depending on the *materials* a building is made of, any or all of these qualities can be downplayed or exaggerated.

with nomadism and other ancient tribal traditions. Hadid can draw on both sources as easily as she can converse in different tongues. She recasts the ancient story of cities in service to her time."

CASA DA MÚSICA (2006),
REM KOOLHAAS (B. 1944)

Rather than attempting to impose order, as architects are traditionally assumed to do, Rem Koolhaas celebrates the randomness of modern life. His buildings are multipurpose, multisensory, contradictory—and often quite startlingly new looking. The cantilevered Seattle Public Library, for instance, looks like no other building you've ever seen. And Koolhaas's Prada stores in New York and Los Angeles, with their multiple levels and interactive dressing rooms, make shoppers as much a part of the buying experience as the clothes. The Pritzker Prize winner is known as one of architecture's most brilliant thinkers, and his books, especially *Delirious New York* (1978) and *S, M, L, XL* (1995), a collaboration with the graphic designer Bruce Mau, are considered some of the most influential writings on design of the past thirty years.

The Casa da Música started out as an answer to a client's request for a living space free of clutter. Koolhaas and his firm, Office of Metropolitan Architecture (OMA), came up with a faceted concrete block with a hollow core. The core was to be the living area, with the spaces around it absorbing the spillover. Nothing came of it, but Koolhaas was loath to give up a good idea. When the city of Porto, in Portugal, announced a design contest for its new concert hall, he adapted his concrete block, and made the hollow core the main auditorium.

Given the Casa da Música's sculptural qualities—it looks like a lopsided cut diamond—it gets a lot of comparisons to **Frank Gehry**'s Guggenheim Museum in Bilbao. The Casa is in fact a much more restrained building. From the outside, it bears a resemblance to the sleek white concrete buildings of Porto's native son, the preeminent modernist Alvaro Siza, himself the holder of a Pritzker Prize. It's only on closer inspection that the Casa da Música's idiosyncrasies are apparent. For one thing, it's the only concert hall in the world with two entirely glass walls. Glass is an acoustical nightmare, but Koolhaas claims to have gotten around this problem by rippling it like a giant curtain and setting the double walls a meter apart to provide noise insulation. But the more startling consequence of the glass is that the auditorium is filled with daylight. And since the glass walls are at opposite ends of the hall, offering views of the skyline from either end, the room seems to be balanced in the very middle of the city. Koolhaas makes references to the surrounding city elsewhere as well, for example in the VIP room, which is lined with Porto's traditional blue and white ceramic tiles. And halfway up the aluminum steps that lead to the main auditorium are two red velvet armchairs that seem to have dropped into the space from another era—as indeed they have, being the work of a now-forgotten Portuguese architect of the 1970s.

FASHION

The archaeologists of the future, said the surrealist artist Jean Cocteau, will learn a great deal about how we lived by looking at our fashion magazines. When Cocteau made his remark, fashion was still a relatively rarefied world, accessible to the few who had the time and money to indulge in its pleasures. Today, fashion is not only a globe-straddling, multibillion-dollar business, it's part of pop culture, as firmly entrenched in the collective imagination as gangster rap or Hollywood blockbusters. Any prospective archaeologist who ignores the fashion magazines of the late twentieth and early twenty-first centuries does so at his or her own peril—as does the culturally ambitious man or woman of today. Everyone recognizes the names of superbrands like Louis Vuitton and Prada, but what about Olivier Theyskens or Comme des Garçons? And even if you've got the means to make a major purchase, do you know a good buy when you see one? With that in mind, this chapter covers the basics that every fashionista's familiar with: who the legends of design are and why their influence lives on, which talents to keep an eye on, and what to wear. It also delves into the more esoteric—and entertaining—aspects of fashion: its muses, oddball visionaries, forgotten idealists, and creative geniuses.

TEN LEGENDS OF TWENTIETH-CENTURY DESIGN

WHAT WOULD MODERN FASHION look like if Coco Chanel hadn't raided her lovers' closets or Claire McCardell hadn't followed through on her conviction that comfort and style weren't mutually exclusive? It's an impossible question to answer, but the influence of these two women—and the eight other designers named here—on what we wear can't be overstated. In the fashion world, they're the names everyone knows.

MADELEINE VIONNET (1876–1975)

Most designers would be dismayed to be known as a dressmaker, a title that suggests that one is capable of the heavy lifting of actually assembling a garment but not gifted with the aesthetic refinement required to envision one. But Madeleine Vionnet, who's often referred to as the greatest dressmaker of the twentieth century, was proud of her draping and cutting skills—justifiably so, for they were the source of

PRONUNCIATION GUIDE
Madeleine Vionnet: **MAD-uh-len vee-oh-NAY**

her innovative designs. While she didn't invent the use of the bias, i.e., cutting fabric diagonally across the weave, she was certainly the first to fully realize the potential of this previously rarely used technique. It was widely adopted by other designers and came to be one of the signature looks of the 1930s. Picture any Depression-era Hollywood starlet in a clinging, icy-white satin gown, her hair peroxided to match, and you've got an idea of how widely Vionnet's artistry was disseminated.

Though cutting on the bias makes fabric more pliable, it also makes it harder to handle. In inexperienced hands, the seams of a bias-cut dress will buckle and ripple and the garment will hang unevenly. In the hands of a master draper and cutter like Vionnet, however, a bias cut is sublime. Her dresses, many of which were inspired by Greek and Roman art, were unhampered by linings or boning and hung limply on the hanger. On the body, however, they followed and highlighted every curve. While never vulgar, they were undeniably sexual, and their unforgiving fits left little to the imagination, a fact that's reflected in the observation Vionnet's most famous for: "When a woman smiles," she said, "her dress should smile with her."

Unlike most designers, who first sketch a design, then draft a paper pattern of their work, and finally put together a cloth version, Vionnet always began with the fabric. Using a two-foot-high wooden mannequin, she would drape and pin the cloth until she achieved the result she wanted. Working in this way, she came to know fabric and its qualities intimately, a knowledge that she exploited fully in her designs.

Though Vionnet closed her house in 1939, her continuing influence on designers who were born years later—John Galliano, for example—is a testament to her talent and vision.

GABRIELLE "COCO" CHANEL (1883–1971)

"L'elégance, c'est moi," said Coco Chanel. Or maybe not. Chanel tossed off so many one-liners in her life that no one's sure what she said and what she didn't. This particular example is grandiose but no more outrageous than the many other bons mots attributed to Mademoiselle—artful lying in the service of her reputation was as much a specialty of the House of Chanel as the use of braided trim or gold chains. In this case, however, her boast actually has a ring of

truth about it. Chanel didn't free women from corsets and long skirts, as she liked to claim. Nor did she invent designer perfume, costume jewelry, or the little black dress, as her legend would have us believe—though she did make spectacularly good use of them. But there's one thing no one doubts: The onetime courtesan who rose from her peasant roots to become the most influential woman in fashion never lacked for elegance. And therein lies her claim to fame. Chanel's genius was to make womenswear elegant by making it more like menswear: She stripped it down, ripped off the furbelows and frills, and made it look clean and modern. Her greatest stroke of luck was being in the right place at the right time, the 1920s—just when women were demanding exactly that from their clothes.

Coco Chanel posed for her friend Man Ray wearing the look that was her trademark: understated clothes, accessorized with scads of real and costume jewelry. And her ever-present cigarette, of course.

Chanel had established her first shop with the backing of two of her lovers in 1913, but it wasn't until the 1920s that she became famous. Her sporty jersey suits, little black dresses that looked like something salesgirls would wear, and sleek evening dresses were christened poverty deluxe because of their frugal air—her skirts were the shortest in Paris—and unconventional fabrics. Before Chanel appropriated it, for example, wool jersey was used only for men's underwear. In the 1930s, Chanel relaxed her style somewhat. Though she had made her reputation as a designer of sportswear, she became known for her romantic tulle-and-lace evening dresses. Even her suits of the time were fitted and conspicuously feminine, nothing like the iconic cardigan suit that her name is now associated with.

The darkest period of Chanel's checkered life came during World War II. A supporter of the right-wing Vichy government, she collaborated with the Nazis, a move that led to a nine-year self-imposed exile in Switzerland after the war ended. She didn't design a collection again until 1954, when, prompted by her dislike of male couturiers such as **Christian Dior**, whom she felt "disfigured" women, she emerged from retirement. Her cardigan suit, with its loose fit and easy-to-wear shape, was a direct reaction to the exaggerated femininity of the postwar years.

Though she had started out as an iconoclast, by the 1960s Chanel had become a fashion dinosaur. She railed against the miniskirt ("Disgusting!") and the trouser suit, refusing to include either in her collections. Her once revolutionary suit became the uniform of the grandes bourgeoises. By the time she died in 1971, the house that Coco built seemed frozen in time, not to be thawed out again until **Karl Lagerfeld** took over creative duties in 1983.

ELSA SCHIAPARELLI (1890–1973)

A series of one-liners or a witty running commentary on fashion, art, and sex? The career of Elsa Schiaparelli tends to spark strong opinions, with few people feeling lukewarm about her work. You either love her irreverence or you think her clothes are weird and you don't get what all the fuss is about.

> **PRONUNCIATION GUIDE**
>
> **Elsa Schiaparelli:**
> **EL-sa SKAP-a-relli**

Born into an aristocratic family in Rome, Schiaparelli was a rebel from an early age. As a teenager, she wrote and published a book of erotic poetry. Her scandalized family promptly exiled her to a convent, though they clearly didn't realize whom they were dealing with—Schiaparelli refused to eat until they let her out.

She was in her thirties before she got involved with fashion, and then it was because she needed money. She'd made a spur-of-the-moment marriage to a Theosophist count named William de Wendt de Kerlor, who'd disappeared and left her with a child (named Gogo) to support. She was leading rich Americans on shopping tours of Paris when she decided to try her hand at design.

With no training or interest in the methodology of fashion, Schiaparelli was never a virtuoso technician, like **Vionnet**, or a hands-on fitter and stylist, like **Chanel**. To her, fashion was an extension of her artistic nature. She didn't concern herself with making pretty frocks or sweet little suits. Instead, she saw dress in terms of unbridled self-expression and bold statements. Her ideas leaned toward the bizarre and the shocking—in fact, "shocking" was a favorite term of hers, and the name of both her perfume and her autobiography. She made an evening dress decorated with the image of a giant steamed lobster garnished with parsley, gloves with appliquéd red fingernails, a telephone-shaped handbag, and a necklace made of aspirin. Her most subversive pieces were the result of her collaborations with Salvador Dalí, whose **surrealist** agenda she shared. Among these was the famous shoe-shaped hat of 1937, which took the sexual connotations and phallic shape of the high heel and made them blatant. The hat was intended to be worn with a suit that had slash pockets appliquéd to look like pink lips, thereby suggesting a relationship between the phallic hat and the feminine lips, which of course are also suggestive of female genitals. While all this would be remarkable enough on the runway today, in the '30s it was, well, shocking.

But Schiap, as she was known, liked to display her flights of fancy against fairly sedate backgrounds, and her brand of hard chic was much in demand. As she wrote in her autobiography, her "greatest fans were the ultra-smart and conservative women, wives of diplomats and bankers, millionaires and artists, who liked severe suits and plain black dresses."

Although she's not copied outright, the way some of her contemporaries are, Schiaparelli's sense of humor and her wit ensure that she'll be remembered long after the clothes of more conventional designers are forgotten.

CRISTÓBAL BALENCIAGA (1895–1972)

In the postwar years, those who followed fashion liked to consider the question of who was the greater designer: **Dior** or Balenciaga? Though both were acclaimed, they were actually quite different.

Dior was a hopeless romantic, forever considering ways to make women look beautiful. Balenciaga was severe, even abstract. An austere elegance, never mere prettiness, was his trademark. For his part, Dior made no secret that he considered Balenciaga the master. "Haute couture is like an orchestra whose conductor is Balenciaga. We other couturiers are musicians and we follow the directions he gives," he said. Because Balenciaga rarely said anything—he gave only one interview to the press in his entire life—we don't know what he thought. His posthumous reputation, however, is secure: Among the cognoscenti, he's considered the greatest designer of the twentieth century.

PRONUNCIATION GUIDE

**Cristóbal Balenciaga:
chris-TOW-ball
ba-lehn-cee-AH-ga**

The son of a dressmaker, Balenciaga studied with his mother from the time he was a child. By the age of twenty, he had opened a tailoring business in his native San Sebastián, Spain, which then evolved into a couture business based in Madrid and Barcelona. But it wasn't until he arrived in Paris, the center of the fashion world, in 1937, that he started on the path to international acclaim.

For those accustomed to the body-conscious fit and flat-out sex appeal of modern design, it may be difficult to understand the appeal of Balenciaga's figure-shrouding dresses. But it's important to remember that high fashion in the 1950s and early '60s was not aimed at twenty-five-year-olds. The small group of women who could afford to buy couture originals were more mature—and in 1950, the average forty-five-year-old looked considerably older than she does today. This sophisticated group loved Balenciaga not only for the conceptual purity of his designs but for his ability to flatter less-than-perfect figures.

This flattery was due to Balenciaga's architectural approach to design. Thanks to his master tailoring, his clothes were truly three-dimensional, forming forgiving spheres, tubes, and pyramids around the body. A narrow skirt, for example, might be capped with a voluminous chemise. To create these sculptural shapes, he chose correspondingly toothsome fabrics—silk gazar, crisp taffetas, thick wools, and beefy velvets. Though his clothes could appear avant-garde, Balenciaga loved traditional Spanish dress and culture, frequently working references to both into his designs. His court-style evening dresses of the late 1930s, for example, recall the portraits of Velázquez, while his capelets and bolero jackets suggest the toreador.

A perfectionist, Balenciaga closed his doors in 1968 rather than continue working in an industry that he considered had lost its way.

CLAIRE McCARDELL (1905–1958)

Practical. Functional. Comfortable. Claire McCardell's clothes are damned by the praise that was lavished on them, all of which sounds disagreeably worthy for a fashion designer. But don't let the blameless adjectives turn you off. McCardell was a realist, but she was also a prodigiously talented visionary whose modernist sympathies and keen understanding of the human form led to clean-lined, sophisticated, slightly edgy clothes that were years, sometimes decades, ahead of their time. Though she didn't invent what became known as "the American look," her casually elegant style exemplified it. Moreover, her scrupulously democratic attitude and problem-solving approach to fashion made her a uniquely American designer. She spent her career on Seventh Avenue, making ready-to-wear clothes at accessible prices, and she believed passionately in good design. "I belong to a mass-production country where any of us, all of us, deserve the right to good fashion and where fashion must be available to all," she once said.

In keeping with this red-white-and-blue ideology, McCardell shunned expensive fabrics in favor of less-obvious cottons, denims, and jerseys. She used these in nontraditional ways, cutting backless halter-top evening dresses from Madras cotton and unlined—and mildly scandalous—bathing suits from jersey. Signature McCardellisms were metal closures, such as brass hooks and eyes; adjustable drawstring necklines and waists; menswear detailing; double rows of topstitching; sashes and yards-long spaghetti ties that could be wrapped and fastened in a variety of ways, thus letting the wearer customize the fit of a dress; large patch pockets; hoods; and empire waists. Never one to succumb to trends, McCardell ignored the broad-shouldered, narrow-skirted silhouette of the 1940s. Instead, her clothes presaged **Dior**'s New Look, with soft shoulders, trim waists, and full skirts. But while Dior built his strict silhouettes on complicated underpinnings, McCardell cut her clothes to follow the curves of the body; she even forbade her models from wearing girdles and pointy bras and taught them to walk with a leggy gait.

Her greatest tribute came from her former colleague Norman Norell: "I worked in the couture tradition—expensive fabrics, hand stitching, exclusivity, all that—but Claire would take five dollars' worth of common cotton calico and turn out a dress a smart woman would wear anywhere."

CHRISTIAN DIOR (1905-1957)

It's a moment that has gone down in fashion history: **Carmel Snow**, the editor of *Harper's Bazaar,* after seeing Christian Dior's inaugural collection in February 1947, embraced him and exclaimed, "It's quite a revolution, dear Christian. Your dresses have such a new look!" Though Dior had named his debut effort Corolla, for the whorl of a petal before it opens, Snow's more prosaic moniker—the New Look—stuck.

But there wasn't anything very new about the clothes Dior had made. The designer acknowledged that, Proust-like, he had been inspired by the sumptuous designs of the belle epoque. Long skirts and narrow waists had popped up in various collections, notably **Balenciaga**'s, since the end of the war. But Dior's timing was impeccable, and his designs were justifiably gorgeous. In contrast to the mannish tailoring of the preceding years, his skirts were long and lush, using up to sixteen yards of fabric; his shoulders rounded; and his waists alluringly small, all details that tapped into an unconscious desire for luxury and femininity. Critics who railed against its extravagances—in the U.K., where clothing, fuel, and food were still rationed, the Labor government considered passing legislation to control hemlines—misread the public mood. After years of privation, women were starved for beauty. Which isn't to say that things didn't occasionally get ugly. During one photo shoot, set in a street market in Montmartre to capture some authentic Paris atmosphere, vendors attacked the models, beating them and tearing their clothes.

From 1947 until his death, Dior remained the most influential designer in the world, his name synonymous with beautiful clothes. Fashion magazines worshipped him, and even newspapers and general-interest magazines covered him the way they would any other world leader. His habit of creating and naming new silhouettes for each season—the H-line, the A-line, the Y-line—became accepted fashion dogma, adding to the perception that male designers controlled gullible women. In fact, Dior was a sensitive and gentle man, so intensely shy that he couldn't bear to watch his shows. He rarely went out and spent as much time as possible at his house in the country. He died there in 1957, at the height of his career.

RUDI GERNREICH (1922-1985)

By 1962, after a dozen years in the business, Rudi Gernreich had established a reputation as one of fashion's wittiest iconoclasts. Cultured and refined, with a knack for divining which way the cultural wind was going to blow, the

PRONUNCIATION GUIDE

**Rudi Gernreich:
ROO-dee gern-RICK**

Vienna-born, Los Angeles–based designer delighted in making titillating statements, the more outrageous the better. So when he told a reporter that "bosoms will be uncovered in five years," it made headlines. Two years later, he cut short his original prediction and, egged on by **Diana Vreeland**, produced the topless bathing suit. A waist-high black brief made racier by the between-the-breasts position of its straps, this now-iconic garment produced a furor that is difficult to imagine in our unbuttoned age (the designer's 1985 "pubikini," a thong that offered a naughty glimpse of pubic hair, never attained quite the same notoriety). Governments from the Vatican to the Kremlin denounced Gernreich as an immoral pornographer. More presciently, recognizing a cultural landmark when they saw it, a group of Italians put it in a time capsule, along with the birth-control pill and a copy of the Bible.

But Gernreich was far more than a one-shock wonder. From his earliest days in fashion, he was determined to produce clothes that were comfortable and practical, like those of his idol, **Claire McCardell**. But McCardell had been working in the 1940s and '50s. In the heady atmosphere of the sexual revolution, Gernreich was able to push boundaries that McCardell had never approached. His unlined bathing suits (some with clear vinyl panels), lightweight T-shirt minidresses, stretch jumpsuits, techno fabrics, unisex styling, and brighter-than-bright colors heralded the future. Worn by the angular, raccoon-eyed Peggy Moffitt, his favorite model and muse, they looked like **pop art** come to life. Just as audacious was his soft no-bra bra of 1965, which jettisoned the nose-cone stitching and truss-work of the postwar brassiere and paved the way for more comfortable, natural-looking styles.

But Gernreich was always more of an artist than a businessman. At the height of his fame, in 1968, a year after *Time* magazine declared him the most influential designer in America, he walked away. When he came back, his career had lost its momentum. Though he continued to experiment, he no longer had the public's attention. Still, he seemed philosophical about his losses and didn't complain that fashion had let him down. "I felt I had to be experimental at any cost," he said soon after leaving fashion to hang out in **Morocco**. "And that meant always being on the verge of a success or a flop."

HALSTON (1932–1990)

Though the early '70s have a reputation for being stylistically confused, with women sporting everything from hot pants to retro fantasies inspired by films such as *The Damned*, the period also saw the emergence of a new minimalism in fashion. And no one did that better than Halston. Nicknamed Mr. Clean, Roy Halston Frowick, whose penchant for stripping things down to the essentials extended to his name, was the champion of tidy but sexy American sportswear. But it was really only after his death, when fashion caught up with his simple-but-luxurious aesthetic, that it became clear how far his influence extended.

He started his career as a milliner in the mid-1950s. By the late '60s, the market for hats was shrinking dramatically, and Halston, who'd been advising his well-heeled clientele about what to wear for years, decided to make the leap to clothes. As a fashion designer, his specialty was taking the classics and updating them without losing any of the qualities that made them classic. He elongated the cashmere twinset into a floor-length dress and coat, for example, and took the shirtwaist dress and cut it from a glamorous new fabric called Ultrasuede. He didn't change his silhouette or his ideas radically from season to season; instead, he stuck with what he knew was both flattering and elegant, like bias-cut evening dresses that knotted at the bust, kimono-inspired coats, and jersey separates. His designs were soft and flowing, never constrictive.

As is perhaps inevitable for someone who palled around with the jet set, it's impossible to separate Halston the designer from Halston the social butterfly. He appears in practically every photo ever taken at **Studio 54**, as well as in two *New Yorker* cartoons, a couple of pop songs, and the ever-memorable fashion-designer episode of the *Love Boat*. Americans in the 1970s weren't nearly as fashion-savvy as they are today, but everyone knew who Halston was. With this in mind, in 1982 JCPenney initiated an agreement with the designer to produce women's, men's, and children's clothes for its shops. As he was already licensing his name to make everything from luggage to bedsheets, Halston thought it was a great idea. It was a deal that ultimately saw him lose control of his name, but like so much of what he did, it foreshadowed the direction fashion was moving in.

YVES SAINT LAURENT (B. 1936)

From his media-frenzy runway shows to his famous dressing of both bride and groom for the Bianca-Mick nuptials, the Yves Saint Laurent of the 1970s, a velvet-clad aesthete who never went anywhere without an entourage—which often consisted of his chic sidekicks Les Fideles, a.k.a. Loulou de la Falaise, Betty Catroux, and Catherine Deneuve—seemed like the ultimate jet-setting designer.

But in January of 1958, when he shot to overnight fame, Yves Saint Laurent was a painfully shy mama's boy of twenty-one. Three months earlier he had been one of several assistants to **Christian Dior,** the most famous designer in the world. In October of that year, Dior died unexpectedly; a month later, Saint Laurent was appointed to take his place and design the spring collection. Though it sounds like a recipe for disaster, it was the first triumph of what was to be a stellar career: Saint Laurent received the sort of rapturous reviews that designers dream about.

His star status with Dior didn't last long, however. His 1960 Left Bank collection, which featured youth-culture staples such as black leather jackets (albeit with mink collars) and turtleneck sweaters, outraged the house's establishment clientele. Its financial backers insisted Saint Laurent go. Following a disastrous compulsory stint in the army, where he had a nervous breakdown, in 1962 he established his own couture house with his longtime boyfriend, Pierre Bergé.

The Left Bank collection proved a harbinger of what was to come, both for Saint Laurent and for fashion. It was the first, but certainly not the last time street style was shown on the runway. For Saint Laurent, this was to prove a persistent theme. Throughout the 1960s and early '70s, his most creative period, he used street fashion as the starting point for his collections, most pointedly in Rive Gauche, the ready-to-wear line he launched in 1966. Menswear references made frequent appearances in his collections: Saint Laurent was one of the first designers to put trousers on his runway, and his famous safari suits and tuxedos *(le smoking)* were both adapted from men's wardrobes, though their erotic appeal when worn by women was well documented by photographer **Helmut Newton**. The arts were another major source of inspiration for Saint Laurent, providing the impetus for some of his most famous looks, including his 1976 rich-hippie Ballets Russes collection. Saint Laurent retired in 2002; the Rive Gauche collection has since been designed by Tom Ford (2002–2004) and Stefano Pilati (2004–present).

VIVIENNE WESTWOOD (B. 1941)

The orange-haired doyenne of British fashion has never been one to care what anyone thinks, a freedom that's made her not just a designer but a one-woman fashion force who's had an astounding impact on the styles of the past thirty-five years. In 1971, dressed in tight leopard-print pedal pushers, ankle socks, and stilettos (her hair was then a spiky platinum), she and her partner, Malcolm McLaren, opened a shop called Let It Rock on London's Kings Road. They sold tailored, 1950s-inspired clothes that represented a feisty, working-class backlash to the hippie movement. Though the shop underwent various name changes over the next decade, each one was perfectly in line with the youth culture of the moment. There was Too Fast to Live, Too Young to Die (1972), a black-leather-jacket-filled biker emporium. That was followed by Sex (1974) and Seditionaries (1977), which sold the rubber corsets, bondage trousers, and other fetish gear that the **punk** movement, encouraged by McLaren (who was by then managing the Sex Pistols), was appropriating. Westwood and McLaren parted ways in 1980, but she held on to the shop, christened it World's End, and used it to showcase her designs, including the seminal Pirates collection, whose many-buckled boots can still be seen on trendsetters like Kate Moss.

By the early 1980s, Westwood had outgrown punk (she's now distanced herself from it completely) and was beginning to explore the historic fashions that continue to fascinate her. Eighteenth-century sack dresses, Victorian bustles and crinolines, and New Look suits have all appeared on her runway, altered by her signature naughtiness—she was the designer who created the mini-crini and put Naomi Campbell in platform shoes so high that the supermodel stumbled and fell during a show. Most winking of all are Westwood's interpretations of traditional Britishisms such as tartans and Harris tweed (a name she borrowed for one of her collections). "I am never more happy than when I parody the British in the context of a classical perspective," she once observed. She was nevertheless given the Order of the British Empire from Queen Elizabeth in 1992, which she went to Buckingham Palace to receive. In typical Westwood fashion, she neglected to wear any underwear to the ceremony.

A true original, Westwood is one of fashion's most fearless thinkers, often years ahead of her peers, as was demonstrated by a retrospective of her work at London's Victoria and Albert Museum in 2004. The exhibit featured the many trends that she's started: customized T-shirts, tube skirts, corsets, and bras worn as outerwear, slashed and printed denim, and fetish wear. Though her look is now so instantly recognizable that it's moved beyond fashion, designers as varied as Alexander McQueen, **Rei Kawakubo**, and Marc Jacobs continue to reference her.

FIVE UNDER-THE-RADAR TALENTS

WHILE NOT THE HOUSEHOLD NAMES the big guns of fashion are, these five designers are known to the cognoscenti for their inventive contributions—each a snapshot of its era—to women's wardrobes.

MADAME GRÈS (1903-1993)

She started out calling herself Alix, then switched to Madame Grès; neither name was her own, but Parisian Germaine Barton, as she was really named, hated the one she was born with. Starting in the 1930s, the onetime sculptor became famous for her neoclassical draped and pleated dresses. The fluid, columnar gowns were reminiscent of the Nike of Samothrace, but they had a sophistication that made them synonymous with the Noel Coward era. Fashion legend has trapped Grès in this period like a moth in amber, but she resurrected her career after the Second World War, and kept mak-

PRONUNCIATION GUIDE

**Madame Grès:
ma-DAM GREH**

ing her timeless clothes, always cut with the female body in mind, straight into the 1980s. Never at the top of the fashion charts, she was nevertheless one of the century's design geniuses.

VALENTINA (1904–1989)

From the late 1920s to the late '50s, the flamboyant Russian émigré Valentina Sanina dressed a select group, never more than two hundred at a time, of the chicest women in America. Her style was one of exquisite simplicity: She cut soberly colored gowns, many with a medieval flavor, from the most gorgeous matte jerseys and velvets she could find, and deigned that they be worn with only the most refined of accessories ("You want bows? You go Macy's," she barked at one client in her heavily accented English). She dressed many actresses, most famously Greta Garbo, who presumably sympathized with her dramatic temperament and flair for epigrammatic outbursts ("Meenk is for football!" "Children are for suburbs!"). One of the only true American couturiers, Valentina closed her business in 1957.

CHARLES JAMES (1906–1978)

Though he was lavishly praised by his contemporaries (**Dior** and **Balenciaga** were fervid admirers, and both **Chanel** and **Schiaparelli** wore his clothes) and his designs were seen on some of the most famous and fashionable women in the world, by the time the Anglo-American couturier Charles James died in a cluttered room at the Chelsea Hotel, he had largely been forgotten. But then for James, whose salad days were the 1950s, the clothes came first, and the women who wore and paid for them second, a business strategy that pretty much guaranteed limited success. He's best known for his architecturally conceived evening gowns, which were so impressively seamed that they stood up on their own, and his extreme devotion to his craft—he once spent three years and thousands of dollars perfecting a sleeve.

OSSIE CLARK (1942–1996)

British-born Ossie Clark's client list read like a who's who of London in the 1960s: Penelope Tree, Twiggy, Bianca Jagger, and Marianne Faithfull all wore his flowing, fairy-princess designs. He was a master tailor, turning silk chiffon and crepe—all printed with nature-inspired designs created by his wife, textile artist Celia Birtwell—into seductive pieces that combined a romantic, Pre-Raphaelite prettiness with the street-theater exuberance of the decade. His runway shows were correspondingly wild, more like rock concerts than fashion presentations. At one, the models had to be pulled off the runway; they were having too good a time dancing to make an exit. Whether you were a rock star's girlfriend or just wanted to look like one, Ossie was your man.

> **PRONUNCIATION GUIDE**
>
> **Ossie Clark:**
> **OZ-zee CLARK**

STEPHEN SPROUSE (1953–2004)

He interned with Bill Blass and worked as **Halston**'s assistant, but fellow Hoosier Stephen Sprouse was always more downtown than uptown. In the late '70s and early '80s, he hung out with **Andy Warhol** (who was buried in a Sprouse suit), dressed Debbie Harry of **Blondie** (she was a neighbor), and spent his nights at the **Mudd Club**, the **new wave** answer to **Studio 54**. But while undeniably talented and a favorite of fellow designers, Sprouse was never a commercial success. Much to his dismay, his neon-bright, graffiti-covered clothes were judged too edgy for mainstream consumers. Sprouse did, however, enjoy a brief period in the fashion spotlight in 2000 as the designer of Louis Vuitton's much-coveted graffiti handbags.

FIVE DESIGNERS' DESIGNERS

FASHION INSIDERS WEAR the big-name brands everyone's heard of—Prada, Marc Jacobs, Louis Vuitton—but they also take professional pride in sporting ones that only other insiders would recognize, like these five.

AZZEDINE ALAÏA (B. 1940)

In the 1980s, Tunisian-born Azzedine Alaïa was every fashion editor's and model's darling. From his studio in the Marais district of Paris, the puckish Alaïa turned out some of the tightest, sexiest clothes ever made, all constructed with lingerie techniques such as crisscross seaming for a fit that didn't just highlight the body but shaped and molded it. These were accented with waist-cinching belts, studded leather gloves, and kinky shoes, turning women into what former Paris *Vogue* editor Joan Juliet Buck called "highly sexualized versions of Darth Vader." The Alaïa look was very

PRONUNCIATION GUIDE
Azzedine Alaïa: **AZZ-uh-deen a-LIE-ah**

severe, very French, and very influential: The fad for stretch minis, biking shorts, and bodysuits all originated on his cutting table. Alaïa, whose sculpting and fitting techniques owe a debt to **Madeleine Vionnet**, never stopped working, but his fame was eclipsed when fashion entered an androgynous phase in the 1990s. He's now back in a big way, worn by trendsetters such as **Carine Roitfeld** and referenced by every young designer in the business.

REI KAWAKUBO (B. 1942)

Comme des Garçons, the label Rei Kawakubo founded in Tokyo in 1975, came into being at a particularly creative juncture in Japanese fashion—her contemporaries are Issey Miyake and Yohji Yamamoto. When the three started showing in Paris in the early 1980s, their seemingly shapeless "bag lady" clothes confused a fashion press accustomed to the conventions of Seventh Avenue and the rue Cambon. Kawakubo's stark, deconstructed designs, like the 1982 sweaters that purposely included rips and holes, are not for the faint of intellect—her collections are meditations on everything from the meaning of identity to the place of religion in modern society. Which is not to say that her clothes are unwearable; they just require a bit more thought than pulling on a pair of jeans. As the designer has said, they're for people who like to take risks. Kawakubo further pushes her vision of fashion with her boutiques, both the permanent kind and the temporary "guerrilla" variety, and in London's Dover Street Market, a six-story style medina that stocks cutting-edge design from around the world.

> **PRONUNCIATION GUIDE**
>
> **Rei Kawakubo:**
> **RAY kah-wah-KOO-bow**

MARTIN MARGIELA (B. 1957)

The reclusive Martin Margiela is so publicity shy that few people know what he looks like (when his design team was photographed in 2001, he was represented by an empty chair). He never gives interviews and is rarely seen in public. But this lack of access has done nothing to hinder Margiela's reputation as one of the most inventive designers in the business. He arrived in Paris from Antwerp in 1982 and spent five years working for Jean Paul Gaultier before setting out on his own in 1989. Lampooning the excesses of fashion was a defining char-

> **PRONUNCIATION GUIDE**
>
> **Martin Margiela:**
> **MAR-tin mahr-JZHEE-el-la**

acteristic of Belgian fashion in the late 1980s, but Margiela excelled at it, making clothes out of recycled Army socks, old ball gowns, and lining fabric. He's still far from complacent, but underneath the high-concept experiments, Margiela is an expert tailor: His suits and jackets are among the best you'll ever find. Hermès, whose clothing line he once designed, would never have hired him if they weren't.

RAF SIMONS (B. 1968)

Like Hedi Slimane, who rose to fame as the creative talent behind Dior Homme, Raf Simons is known primarily as a menswear designer. But female fans of Simons's pure Northern tailoring don't have to resort to buying his men's clothes, as did the fair number of women who shopped at Dior Homme when Slimane was there. Since the fall of 2006,

> **PRONUNCIATION GUIDE**
>
> **Raf Simons:**
> **RAFE SIM-mons**

Simons has been designing both the women's and men's lines at Jil Sander, a label renowned for its luxurious minimalism. Perhaps because Simons is a self-taught fashion designer (he trained as an industrial designer), he doesn't ascribe to fashion-world hype. His clothes solve real problems—what to wear to work, how to make a dress look modern—without looking boringly basic. A quiet rebel who pushes "pride in individuality," Simons's references are often drawn from youth-culture tribes such as mods or punks, though these are more a spiritual affinity than a literal interpretation—he's much too subtle a designer to do anything so obvious.

TIP SHEET

WHO DESIGNS WHAT

• Anne Klein is designed by Isabel Toledo. • **Balenciaga** is designed by Nicolas Ghesquière. • Balmain is designed by Christophe Decarnin. • Bill Blass is designed by Peter Som • Bottega Veneta is designed by Tomas Maier. • Burberry Prorsum is designed by Christopher Bailey. • Calvin Klein is designed by Francisco Costa. • Celine is designed by Ivana Omazic. • **Chanel** is designed by **Karl Lagerfeld**. • Chloé is designed by Paulo Melim. • **Christian Dior** is designed by John Galliano. • **Comme des Garçons** is designed by **Rei Kawakubo**. • Costume National is designed by Ennio Capasa. • Fendi is designed by Karl Lagerfeld. • Ferragamo is designed by Graeme Black. • Givenchy is designed by Riccardo Tisci. • Gucci is designed by Frida Giannini. • Hermès is designed by Jean Paul Gaultier. • Jil Sander is designed by **Raf Simons**. • Lanvin is designed by Alber Elbaz. • Louis Vuitton is designed by Marc Jacobs. • Marni is designed by Consuelo Castiglioni. • Nina Ricci is designed by **Olivier Theyskens**. • Pucci is designed by Matthew Williamson. • **Yves Saint Laurent** is designed by Stefano Pilati.

• And, finally, Valentino is designed by Valentino, but that's his first name, not his last—that's Garavani. That might not last much longer, though. Mr. Valentino, as he's usually known, is talking about retiring.

OLIVIER THEYSKENS (B. 1977)

PRONUNCIATION GUIDE

Olivier Theyskens:
oh-lee-VEE-ay TAY-skins

Even before Madonna wore his black satin coatdress to the Academy Awards in 1998, Olivier Theyskens was exciting attention in the fashion world. The young Belgian with the mostly black clothes, many adorned with his signature hook-and-eye fastenings, was pegged as a talent to watch, a feeling that reached mass consensus in 2002, when he went to work for the house of Rochas. Despite collections that concentrated on high-end, Edwardian-style gowns (some costing as much as a hundred thousand dollars) to the almost complete exclusion of daywear, Theyskens has emerged as one of the most influential designers of his generation. Evening fabrics worn during the day, covered-up dresses, and a predilection

PRONUNCIATION GUIDE

Nicolas Ghesquière:
nee-koh-LA JESS-kee-air

Balmain: bal-MAYN

Christophe Decarnin:
krees-TOFF de-KAR-nehn

Bottega Veneta:
bow-TAY-ga ven-NUH-ta

Tomas Maier:
THO-mas MY-er

Comme des Garçons:
CUM DAY GAR-sohn

for goth flourishes can all be traced to his atelier. Though Theyskens found himself out of a job when the corporate giant that owned Rochas shut the house down in the summer of 2006, he was quickly scooped up by another Parisian label in need of an image overhaul, Nina Ricci.

FIVE PIECES TO SPEND MONEY ON

CONVENTIONAL WISDOM HOLDS that the bulk of your clothing budget should be spent on shoes and handbags because they'll make your outfit. True, but you should include all your accessories in that category—clothes are generic, it's the details that set you apart—and add a good coat.

A HANDBAG

A handbag is more than just a convenient way to transport your daily necessities. Think of it not as a purely practical purchase but a symbolic one. Fashion people select their bags on the premise that even if they were to run out of their apartments naked during a fire, with no time to grab anything else, they would still be identifiable as fabulous. Which is not to say that a bag should shriek its provenance to the uninitiated—if a designer's name or initials are visible from a distance of ten feet, then it, and by extension you, are trying too hard. "It" bags vary from season to season, but you can reliably flaunt an Hermès Birkin or Kelly, a classic quilted **Chanel** bag with a chain handle, or a woven Bottega Veneta tote. Once you've acquired a suitably impressive bag, carry it casually, as though you think nothing of swinging several thousand dollars' worth of leather from your wrist.

SHOES

Shoes are a fashionista's flirty Ginger Rogers to the more polished, Fred Astaire appeal of a handbag. To paraphrase Katharine Hepburn's quip about the dancing duo, a bag gives you class, shoes give you sex. Not always nice sex, mind you, but sex. Both, naturally, should radiate status. The type of shoe you choose—flats, heels, boots, ankle-strap, sandal, etc.—is a matter of personal taste, and to some extent price is open for discussion (Converse All Stars and Frye boots have both earned nods from the professionally stylish), but your footwear's state of repair should never flag (the only exceptions to this rule are the aforementioned sneakers and boots, which can acquire a slight patina of age). Keep heels from getting run-down, polish leather, and brush suede. The determinedly fashionable often opt for the "difficult" shoe—i.e., one with awkward proportions, an unmanageable height, or a blithe unconcern for the terrain it must negotiate—over the crowd-pleasing pointed-toe/narrow-heel combination, but that can be seen as overkill.

A COAT

What is Kate Moss wearing in practically every single paparazzi photo ever taken of her? A coat or jacket. Along with the standard-issue glam kit of giant shades and a four-figure handbag, Ms. Moss has inevitably got on some sort of memorable topper over her jumper and jeans. If one of the most photographed women in the world acknowledges the worth of good outerwear, who are you to argue? A well-made coat makes you feel instantly pulled together. It also sees a lot of wear and gets far more display time than what goes beneath it, all good reasons to look on it as an investment.

Like Moss, who's actually a fairly classic dresser, it's best to go with the tried-and-true: Trench coats and peacoats, which thanks to their military roots look discreetly aristocratic, will never fail you. Leather jackets, provided they're narrow and close fitting, are another good choice. Choose solid colors over prints, and don't buy anything that doesn't fit in the shoulders.

JEWELRY

The key to impressing via jewelry is to avoid the mundane. A run-of-the-mill solitaire engagement ring? Yawn. Matching earrings and necklace? Uh-uh. Instead, think outside the Tiffany blue box. Remember **Coco Chanel**, who, as **Christian Dior** admiringly observed, "with a black pullover and ten rows of pearls . . . revolutionized fashion." Pearls can be tricky, though—wear them the wrong way and you risk looking like a 1950s matron. If you want to wear pearls, think of Sofia Coppola, who's turned conservative dressing into a hipster statement. Diamonds are a safer bet. Vintage jewels are always good, especially if they have unusual settings—**art deco**, Victorian—and an interesting story behind them. An array of striking pendants worn in clusters suggests that you've spent years unearthing them in obscure vintage shops (always impressive). Rings should be either substantial or stacked. Above all, jewelry should be worn in an individual manner—even if that manner is borrowed from someone else.

SUNGLASSES

Far from being merely a method of keeping the sun out of your eyes, shades are a surefire way to add glamour and sex appeal to your appearance. Consider this: When Tom Ford, the man who made kind-of-louche, kind-of-'70s, definitely sexy the way to dress, retired from Gucci and **Yves Saint Laurent**, one of the first projects he put his name on was a line of sunglasses. Why? Because pretty much anyone looks more impressive in sunglasses, and people will always spend money to look more impressive. Down, sunglasses exaggerate your personal importance by suggesting you're too busy to be approached. Pushed on top of your head, they connote I've-just-stepped-off-my-yacht nonchalance. For no matter how many cancer stats dermatologists wave in admonition, **Coco Chanel**'s sun-kissed South of France legacy still suggests greater riches and privileges than pale but healthy skin. Keep in mind that when it comes to sunglasses, big is good, but ridiculously oversize is merely ridiculous.

TEN OF FASHION'S MOST INFLUENTIAL IMAGE MAKERS

FASHION IS ALL ABOUT creating gorgeous, seductive images, but the clothes are just the start of the process. You cannot, for example, separate YSL's *le smoking* from the moody, sexually charged photographs Helmut Newton took of it. The following are the editors, photographers, art directors, and retailers behind the images that have defined fashion's visual vocabulary.

CARMEL SNOW (1887–1961)

Though she's best remembered as the woman who gave the New Look its name, it's unfair to reduce Carmel Snow to this one comment. The editor in chief of *Harper's Bazaar* from 1933 to 1958 may be overshadowed by her more flamboyant protégée, **Diana Vreeland**, but she was the better editor. Vreeland was a fashion visionary whose flair for the kind of caprices that fashion flourishes on is unmatched, but Snow presided over the more widely interesting publication. In setting out to create a magazine for "the well-dressed woman with the well-dressed mind," Snow determined that her readers were interested in more than just hemlines and hats. She published fiction by **Truman Capote** and Carson McCullers, journalism by Janet Flanner and Katherine Anne Porter, and photography by **Richard Avedon** (who said, "Carmel Snow taught me everything I know") and **Lillian Bassman** and illustrations by **Andy Warhol**. She would do anything for a good story, whether that was wangling one of the first French visas to be granted after the Nazis were ousted in 1944—an epic voyage that resulted in a series of clear-eyed letters home, all duly printed in *Bazaar*—or writing endless flattering notes to writers whose voices she wanted in her pages.

Snow got her start at *Vogue* in the 1920s, but after years of chafing under the authority of Edna Woolman Chase, whose reign there lasted an astonishing thirty-eight years, she jumped ship to the rival publication. In doing so, she broke her word—she'd promised her boss and mentor, Condé Nast, that she'd never work for the publication he considered the enemy. Neither he nor Chase took the move lightly; when Chase spotted Snow at Nast's funeral nine years later, she was incensed.

In going to work for William Randolph Hearst, Snow was by no means guaranteeing herself a rise in prestige. The *Bazaar* of the time was positively dumpy compared with *Vogue* (until Snow hired **Alexey Brodovitch**, that is), and Hearst was notoriously difficult to work for. But Snow relished their clashes. In 1937, she published a photograph of the opera singer Marian Anderson, breaking an unwritten rule that blacks were not to appear in the magazine. Hearst raged, but Snow prevailed.

Bazaar was Snow's life. She married late and had her children in rapid succession. But she and her husband spent time together only rarely, and her three girls were raised by nannies. When she was fired from the magazine she loved, her drinking, which had been something of a legend for years, picked up. She died just a few years after her retirement.

ALEXEY BRODOVITCH (1898–1971)

As the art director of *Harper's Bazaar* from 1934 to 1958, Alexey Brodovitch's influence on the look and feel of the modern fashion magazine is impossible to overstate. When he arrived at *Bazaar*, fashion magazines (with the notable exception of *Vogue,* where art director Dr. Mehemed Fehmy Agha, another émigré, created dynamic pages) would usually crowd several photographs and their accompanying captions onto one page, sometimes against an ornamental background. The effect, even when the models had bobbed hair and short skirts, was one of Victorian fussiness. Brodovitch, with the encouragement of editor in chief **Carmel Snow**, who'd persuaded a hidebound William Randolph Hearst to hire the Russian former cavalry officer, swept all the fuss off the page. He would open stories with what's now a standard magazine technique: a double-page spread. These inevitably featured one striking photograph, often enlarged or unexpectedly cropped; a headline; a block of text—and lots of clean, white, modernist space.

His design philosophy was simple: Acknowledge the vertical fold, leave plenty of open space, and make sure that every page contains an element of surprise. Most important, Brodovitch recognized that modern fashion was as much about lifestyle as it was about clothes. Working with **Diana Vreeland**, *Bazaar*'s fashion editor at the time, he encouraged photographers to be expressionistic. Rather than serving as clotheshorses for buttons and bows, models became characters in a story. In an early shoot by Martin Munkacsi, a model bounds over sand dunes in a striped cape. They were the kind of images that prompted Edna Woolman Chase, the editor of the much stuffier *Vogue,* to opine that *Bazaar* had taken to featuring "farm girls jumping over fences."

A photographer himself, Brodovitch served as mentor to some of the century's most striking fashion photographers, including **Richard Avedon**, **Irving Penn**, Toni Frissell, Louise Dahl-Wolfe, **Lillian Bassman**, and Erwin Blumenfeld. In keeping with *Bazaar*'s wide-ranging editorial policy, Brodovitch commissioned plenty of nonfashion photography as well, including war photos shot by Henri Cartier-Bresson, who said Brodovitch was the only art director whom he allowed to crop his photos.

Brodovitch was sacked from *Bazaar* after twenty-four years of service. His penchant for four-martini lunches may have had something to do with it, but given that Snow was just as summarily dispatched a year later, it's likely that the magazine's publishers wanted a change of direction. They got it: Within a few years, *Bazaar* lost all the elegance Brodovitch had given it. But its midcentury high point wasn't forgotten: When Liz Tilberis took over as editor in chief in 1992, she chose Fabien Baron, who also espouses a stylish **minimalism**, to be her art director. Their first issue, now a collector's item among fashion editors, had a single cover line: "A Return to Elegance."

SIR CECIL BEATON (1904–1980)

Cecil Beaton was an English photographer, writer, illustrator, and set and costume designer. He was also a social climber, a spectacular snob, and, in a career that spanned six decades, one of fashion's most prolific gadabouts. Imagine a more WASPish **Andy Warhol** with a public-school accent and you've got Cecil Beaton.

Even as a child, Beaton's pretensions got the better of him. He grew up in a comfortable middle-class family, but, yearning to belong to a more rarefied strata, he sent photos of his mother—complete with captions suggesting she was a social figure of some importance—to a local paper. Taking the boy at his word, the paper published them. He later played the same trick with his sisters, photographing them as debutantes.

He got his start at British *Vogue* in the 1920s, the decade of the Bright Young Things. Beaton chronicled their doings with his camera and his archly amusing jottings (of the stage actress Gertrude Lawrence he wrote, "She smoked cigarettes with a nuance that implied having just come out of bed and wanting to go back into it"). He was, in the words of Carly Simon, "where you should be all the time," photographing flapper shifts in Condé Nast's lavish New York apartment in the '20s, models in bombed-out London buildings during the war, and a girlish Twiggy in the '60s. He loved photographing royalty (he was rewarded with a knighthood in 1972), with the Queen Mother a particular favorite (he once pocketed her scented hankie as a souvenir of a sitting). He also photographed her American counterpart and rival, the twice-divorced **Duchess of Windsor**, most notably in her wedding dress.

The costumes he designed for *My Fair Lady*—if you've seen the film you'll very likely remember the dramatic black-and-white gowns and enormous hats from the Ascot scene—won him an

Academy Award. But while he pretended to be charmed by the film's star, Audrey Hepburn, his diary, which was published in an unexpurgated version only years after his death, reveals what he really thought. She was, in his opinion, "a troubled sprite in blue dungarees, a citizen Puck" with "homely approachability." That Hepburn got off easy. Of Katharine, he was unsparing. "That beautiful bone structure of cheekbone, nose, and chin goes for nothing in the surrounding flesh of the New England shopkeeper," he sniped. "Her skin is revolting . . . her appearance is appalling, a raddled, rash-ridden, freckled, burnt, mottled, bleached and wizened piece of decaying matter. It is unbelievable, incredible that she can still be exhibited in public." As with many of Beaton's private thoughts, there's a strong hint of misogyny in the venom.

And yet Beaton could make anyone look elegant and soigné. His friend **Truman Capote** may—or may not, given his own history—have been suggesting more than he knew when he said of his pal, "The camera will never be invented that could capture or encompass all that he actually sees."

DIANA VREELAND (C. 1905–1989)

You can't have an interest in fashion and not know who Diana Vreeland is—it's like professing a love for Italian food without ever having tasted pasta. The basics are pretty straightforward: La Vreeland created the role of fashion editor as it's popularly imagined. Which is to say she made outrageous pronouncements, promoted wildly unwearable looks, and cultivated an unabashedly eccentric personality that involved wearing Kabuki-style makeup and spouting fatuous nonsense such as "The bikini is the most important thing since the atom bomb." It's practically impossible to confirm any facts about Vreeland, because she made things up as she went along—insisting, for example, that Buffalo Bill Cody taught her to ride. This much is known: She was born to a socially prominent family, allegedly in Paris, and spent the first thirty-seven years of her life doing not much of anything other than wearing clothes. Her first job was at *Harper's Bazaar,* where she worked for twenty-four years, but it was her stint as the editor in chief of *Vogue* (1962–1971) that let her creative spirit run wild and confirmed her maverick reputation. She swept away everything that was staid about the magazine and devoted page after page to what she termed the Youthquake. Where *Vogue* had once chronicled the lives of society ladies in tailored suits, it was now given over to fantastical pictorials set in exotic locales such as North Africa and the Middle East, the most famous of which showed model Veruschka posing in the desert wearing nothing but miles of fake fur and Dynel hair. But while fashion people adored—and continue to adore—this sort of thing, advertisers weren't so keen, preferring photos that showed clothes you could actually go out and buy. By the early 1970s, something had to give. Vreeland and her spendthrift ways were shown the door and *Vogue* got a lot beiger—and more profitable. She then moved on to the next stage in her career, becoming a special consultant to the Costume Institute at the Metropolitan Museum of Art. There, she produced extravagant shows that were long on romance and short on facts. But this didn't detract the fashion world's greatest oracle and most visionary mythmaker. "Reality is a world as you feel it to be, as you wish it to, as you wish it into being," she said.

LILLIAN BASSMAN (B. 1917)

Though the ranks of fashion writers and editors have always been dominated by women, there have been comparatively few female fashion photographers. There have been some great women fashion photographers—Louise Dahl-Wolfe, for example, who glorified the all-American girl in her color-saturated location shots of the 1940s and '50s, or Deborah Turbeville, whose pensive 1970s heroines have a peculiarly haunting quality—but even today, the best-known names in the field are men.

Lillian Bassman, who made her name at **Carmel Snow**'s *Harper's Bazaar,* is an insider's favorite. Her expressive black-and-white photos don't necessarily show all the "buttons and bows" that Snow demanded, but their tactile delicacy is lovely to behold.

Like so many other photographers, Bassman was helped into fashion by **Alexey Brodovitch**, who hired her as his assistant and then made her the art director of *Bazaar*'s younger sister, *Junior*

Bazaar. It was while she was at *Junior Bazaar* that she made the leap to photography; its final issue, in 1948, carries her first big story.

From the beginning, the self-taught Bassman was interested in experimenting with film. In the darkroom, she printed negatives through layers of gauze to achieve a soft-focus effect and used bleach to lighten and highlight her images. At their most extreme, her photos are practically abstract. A 1951 image is reduced to a few black lines that sketch the outline of a spreading coat, yet these are so graceful that its sweep is easy to see. But even Bassman's more figurative work sings. A 1958 photo of a swan-necked woman turning to face the camera is an elegant study in contrasts, with the velvety blacks of her dress and hat offsetting her luminous skin and the gleam of her diamond earrings.

It's an extraordinarily intimate portrait, as are all Bassman's fashion images. She attributed this to the lack of sexual tension on the set. Unlike her male colleagues, she never felt like she had to seduce her models. Instead, they became friends, and chatted about husbands and boyfriends. A stylish lover of fashion, Bassman would often try the clothes on before the shoot, to get an idea of how they felt.

Bassman retired from commercial photography in the early 1970s. At about the same time, she gave her studio a thorough cleaning and threw out all the negatives from her *Bazaar* years. Or so she thought. In the early '90s, a few turned up under a bench in her darkroom, and she printed them, reinterpreting many as she went. The resulting book brought her new fans—and new assignments. In 1996, she came out of retirement to shoot an advertising campaign for Neiman Marcus and the couture collections for *The New York Times*.

IRVING PENN (B. 1917)

If ever a photographer understood the importance of a cuff or a new way of cutting a skirt, it's Irving Penn. His stark, startling images, often rendered in crisp black-and-white, invest fashion with importance and dignity. They're like artifacts from an archaeological fashion dig, in which the curve of a shoulder or the shape of a heel can be scrutinized for information on the society that produced them.

Penn studied under *Harper's Bazaar*'s **Alexey Brodovitch**, but he made his name at *Vogue*. When the New Jersey–born photographer started shooting for the magazine, in the early 1940s, the image considered suitable for *Vogue*'s pages was one of frosty hauteur. "The ideal setting was a French drawing room," Penn recalled later. "I didn't know what a French drawing room looked or felt like, and the ideal women were remote, with European overtones. . . . I could photograph only what I knew and felt comfortable with. I made pictures in simple circumstances of women I could imagine and want to possess."

That sense of emotional involvement and the erotic frisson that comes with it is most evident in the many photos Penn took of his wife, Lisa Fonssagrives, who was also his favorite model. They were married in 1950, and worked together throughout the decade. Fonssagrives's cool blond beauty was the perfect foil for Penn's academic formality. The best of their work together, like the 1950 photo of her wearing a black-and-white harlequin dress and smoking a cigarette, her eyebrows penciled into quizzical arches, has an electric sassiness and intelligence. Though she referred to herself as merely a "good clothes hanger," the sophistication and wit she brought to her collaborations with Penn are undeniable.

Drama is a hallmark of Penn's photography. His fashion photos turn on the interrupted moment—a 1951 shot of model Jean Patchett lying in bed with her eyes shut, a telephone receiver pressed to her ear, makes you wonder what she's just been told. Drama also reigns in Penn's portraits, many of which feature subjects who've been backed into corners and uncompromisingly lit. Penn's penchant for even, forensically sharp lighting is legendary. Even when he was traveling in New Guinea in 1970, taking photos of indigenous peoples, he wouldn't give up his northern light. He built a portable studio with a skylight and took photos of mask-wearing tribesmen that are as sharp and clear as his renderings of the couture.

Penn gives his meticulously arranged still lifes the same care and attention he gives his fashion and portrait work. Whether he's laying out cigarette butts picked off New York City streets, the green and silver Clinique products he's been shooting since the late 1960s, or the imaginative still lifes he still creates for *Vogue*, his images are never less than pristine.

HELMUT NEWTON (1920-2004)

Helmut Newton liked to say that he wasn't an intellectual and he didn't stand for anything. As the man responsible for some of the most erotically charged photos ever taken, this cheerful who-me stance seems somewhat ingenuous, to say the least. But it leaves his work wide open to interpretation, and there's enough there to keep a battalion of Freudians busy for years. What with the bondage,

The erotic undertones of Yves Saint Laurent's androgynous le smoking are brought to the fore in Helmut Newton's iconic photo, one of the most famous images in fashion.

domination, sadomasochism, fetishism, and voyeurism, there was nothing cozy about Newton's take on fashion. (Or anything else: He once photographed a fried chicken for *Vogue*—but not before fitting it with a pair of miniature high heels.)

He was born Helmut Neustädter to a wealthy Jewish family in Berlin. He was sickly as a child, and his mother cosseted him, dressing him in velvet suits. From this emasculating experience Newton traced his fetish for the strapping Valkyries who would later appear in his photographs (the title *Big Nudes,* a book of his photos, is as good a synopsis as any of his aesthetic). He managed to get out of Germany in 1938, shortly after Kristallnacht, and made his way to Singapore, where he claimed to work as a gigolo. After a spell in Australia, he moved to Paris with his wife and creative partner, June, a photographer who uses the name Alice Springs professionally.

Like a cross between *The Decameron* and the Marquis de Sade, Newton's kinky photos are set among the bored and affluent, frequently in the anonymous environment of a hotel room. The protagonists in these scenarios are almost always women, often nude but for their high heels; men, when they appear, are secondary players. In one of Newton's most famous images, a model in a floral dress sits with her legs apart, idly sizing up an anonymous man in the way that men so often rate passing women. Like all Newton's women, she's splendidly insolent. But this was tame compared to most of his hijinks. He posed women on crutches, in orthopedic corsets, in wheelchairs, and on all fours wearing an Hermès saddle. These Amazonian creatures are never less than completely in charge, but this didn't stop critics from accusing him of demeaning women. In the 1970s outcry over "porno chic," as the work of photographers such as **Guy Bourdin** and Chris von Wangenheim was termed, Newton was the target of frequent polemics from women's groups.

He met his end in a way that you could imagine providing the background narrative for one of his provocative tableaux: As he swung his Cadillac out of the driveway of the **Chateau Marmont** hotel, where he and June wintered, onto Sunset Boulevard, he had a heart attack and crashed into oncoming traffic.

RICHARD AVEDON (1923–2004)

Models never seem to stand still in Richard Avedon's photos. Whether they're laughing, dancing, or, in his most famous shot, *Dovima and the Elephants,* communing with pachyderms while clad in a **Christian Dior** evening gown and opera-length gloves, they're full of character and spirit. And they always seem to be having a good time.

He was discovered in 1945, fresh out of the Merchant Marine, by **Alexey Brodovitch**. Within a year of their meeting, Avedon's photos were appearing in *Harper's Bazaar,* where his infectious enthusiasm and flair for experimentation fit right in with the prevailing mood. The war was over, the future looked bright, and fashion was entering a period of extraordinary creativity and popularization. Avedon's energetic images, which picked up where the leaping farm girls of Martin Munkacsi left off, dramatized this vitality the way no aloof mannequin shot could.

His fascination with fashion dated back to his childhood, when he read fashion magazines the way other boys read comic books and lined the walls of his room with tear sheets of his favorite images. When he became a photographer, this early education in fashion served him well. Whether he was photographing Suzy Parker running down the Champs Elysées in 1950s couture or Penelope Tree tooling around the studio barefoot in bell-bottom trousers in the late 1960s, he instinctively grasped what the bigger picture was. Even when he was shooting against a seamless white background in the studio, the method he came to prefer, he always managed to convey what was going on in the wider world and how fashion fit into it.

To the public, Avedon epitomized his profession, a perception that was confirmed when he was the inspiration for the character of Dick Avery, a photographer played by Fred Astaire, in the fashion love letter *Funny Face*. The film also featured Dorothy Virginia Margaret Juba as a model with a flair for extravagant poses. Better known by the alias she created for herself out of the first syllables of her given names, she was the girl with her gloved hand on an elephant's trunk in *Dovima and the Elephants*.

Avedon's portraits, for which be became as famous as his fashion work, are deceptively simple. He photographed his subjects straight on, against the inevitable white background, with even lighting, and usually in black-and-white. But rather than giving them a sameness, this framework makes their humanity and individuality all the more apparent. Whether he was photographing famous figures such as Jacqueline Kennedy or the motley crowd at the Factory (a series of photos that inspired the Calvin Klein ads of the 1990s), he recognized their dignity.

In 1992, Avedon was hired as the first staff photographer for *The New Yorker,* a magazine that had previously been suspicious of photography, with the promise that he could shoot anything he wanted. He was on assignment for them when he died.

GUY BOURDIN (1928–1991)

In the 1970s, when he was photographing extensively for Paris *Vogue,* Guy Bourdin was sent to Tahiti for two weeks to do a bathing-suit shoot for the magazine. All he came back with was a single image, of a row of naked models with red anthuriums protruding from between their legs, not a bikini in sight. The stunt was emblematic of both Bourdin's trying personality and his photographic style, which combined sex, beauty, and a finely wrought sense of the perverse into one burnished, disturbing package that's left a permanent kink in fashion and advertising imagery.

PRONUNCIATION GUIDE

**Guy Bourdin:
GHEE boor-DIHN**

Though there's no such thing as a typical Bourdin photo—a random selection of the images he produced over the years includes a high-heel sandal lying by the side of the road in front of a wrecked car, from one of the many ad campaigns he shot for the shoe designer Charles Jourdan; a woman on horseback attacking a man with her riding crop; a nude model lying on her stomach with a pool of shiny red liquid spilling from her lipsticked mouth—there are certain consistencies that mark his wholly original eye. A sense of the inexplicable; an obsessive tidiness that verges on the demented; a hard, high-gloss finish; saturated color, whether of the water in a pool or the blush on a model's cheek; and an overriding sense of menace are all signature Bourdinisms. It's the last that's the most striking. Try as you might, there's no way to imagine a happy ending to the scenarios he so carefully crafted. And "crafted" is the right word—unlike his stylistic descendant David LaChapelle, Bourdin worked in the days before digital cameras and Photoshop. His heightened, alternate-reality images relied solely on a combination of meticulously constructed sets, props, and makeup, all masterfully lit. But Bourdin, a perfectionist who would have preferred to have been a painter, was never satisfied, which is perhaps why he never allowed his work to be collected in a book or exhibited in galleries.

A look at the photographer's tortured private life suggests that there's a significant subplot to his disdain for his work (and, indeed, for why he chose to toil in such a relentlessly insecure field as fashion). Abandoned by his mother as a baby, he saw himself as a doomed figure. His first wife may have killed herself; his second certainly did. Not surprisingly, his attitude to his work was so cavalier that by the time he died, this once lionized photographer was almost entirely forgotten. It's only in the past few years that Bourdin's reputation has been resurrected and the importance of his work once again recognized.

BARBARA HULANICKI (B. 1936)

In the late 1950s, fashion was for older women. Those who could afford it bought straight from Paris, from whence all fashion originated; everyone else wore whatever their local department stores chose to copy from the Paris collections. If you didn't want to dress like your mother, you were out of luck. Barbara Hulanicki, then a young fashion artist, remembers "looking forward to the day when I would be that old and could cope with all the elegance." As it happened, Hulanicki never had to face that eventuality. In 1964,

> **PRONUNCIATION GUIDE**
>
> **Biba:**
> **BEE-ba**

emboldened by the success of a few dresses they'd sold via the post, she and her husband, Stephen Fitz-Simon, opened their first shop in an old pharmacy on Abingdon Road in West London. They called it Biba, after Hulanicki's younger sister, and they sold one kind of dress, in one

WHO THE KEY IMAGE MAKERS ARE NOW

Maverick English stylist/*Pop* magazine editor **Katie Grand** cut her teeth at legendary style bible *The Face*. She now consults for the Prada, Miu Miu, and Louis Vuitton runway shows each season, where her myriad references keep things bubbling. • Self-described fashion nymphomaniac, all-around culture junkie, and master of the sound bite **Karl Lagerfeld**, a.k.a. the Kaiser, designs **Chanel** and Fendi as well as his own line and in 2004 produced a sold-out collection for H&M. • You'll rarely see a photo of her, but it's publicity-shy **Sarah Lerfel**'s far-seeing taste that makes Colette, the perennially hip lifestyle boutique on Paris's rue St. Honoré, an essential stop on the international fashion circuit. • Known for her untamed eyebrows and face-covering fall of dark hair, the fiercely chic Paris *Vogue* editor in chief **Carine Roitfeld** was the stylist who helped turn Gucci into one of the most successful labels of the 1990s. • Few designers will send a model (female or male) out on the runway without the prior ministrations of makeup artist **Pat McGrath**. Working with her frequent collaborator hairstylist Eugene Souleiman, she creates looks that range from the barely there to Bollywood theatricality. • Photographer and frequent contributor to the American and Italian editions of *Vogue* **Steven Meisel** doesn't shy away from controversy. He shot both the borderline pornographic Calvin Klein underwear ads and his pal Madonna's *Sex* book. • **Suzy Menkes**, the pompadoured chief fashion reporter for the *International Herald Tribune*, is one of the most respected journalists in the business—for her services to fashion, she's been made a Chevalier of the Legion of Honor. • **Carla Sozzani**, sister of Italian *Vogue* editor Franca Sozzani, presides over 10 Corso Como in Milan, one of the best-curated boutiques in the world (if you want more of her impeccable taste, stay in 3Rooms, her adjacent hotel). • Peruvian-born photographer **Mario Testino** has an incredible knack for making people look good.

print. Within an hour of opening, every last one was gone. The Biba phenomenon was under way.

From the first, Hulanicki understood what her contemporaries wanted: clothes that looked and felt young and that could be bought on a working girl's wages. She designed for the minxes of 1960s London, "fresh little foals with long legs, bright faces and round dolly eyes." She gave them simple cuts, short hems, and what she called "Auntie colors": the deep plums, dusky blueberries, and murky mauves of a freshly blooming bruise. Just as important, she gave them a place to congregate. With its dark interior, **art nouveau** decor, and loud music, Biba felt more like a club than a store. Hulanicki not only made fashion accessible, she transformed shopping from a chore to what we know it as today: a pastime.

Though Biba's prices were low, it quickly became a celebrity haunt. Mick Jagger kept an account for each of his girlfriends; when they broke up, he stopped paying their bills. By the early 1970s, Biba had become all encompassing, selling everything from diapers (dyed purple, of course) to lipstick (sepia was the preferred shade). Its final incarnation, in a 1930s-era department store, was a camp-meets-**art deco** fairy tale of a shop, with the famed Biba logo in black and gold over the front door and a roof garden that over-flowed with flowers and pink flamingos. The fairy tale came to an end, as so many fashion ones do, when Hulanicki and Fitz-Simon had creative differences with their backers. In 1974, Biba closed its doors. There have been numerous attempts to revive it since, most recently with the appointment of the English designer Bella Freud—a daughter of the painter **Lucian Freud**—as creative director.

FIVE WOMEN WHO DESIGNERS LOVE TO REFERENCE

FORGET AUDREY HEPBURN—designers have a far more select group of women whose style they like to pay homage to. Knowing who these women are is a key element to understanding fashion, especially since fashion people tend to use their names as shorthand reference points—"that show was very Edie"—all the time.

MARCHESA LUISA CASATI (1881-1957)

With her aureole of flaming red hair, enormous, kohl-ringed eyes, and cadaverous face, the Marchesa Luisa Casati was easy to spot. Add the pair of cheetahs on diamond-studded leashes that she liked to take for walks around Venice, her habit of appearing in public naked under her fur coat, and the nude, gilded male servants who waited on her and you begin to see why she was known as the most decadent woman in the world (and why Dita Von Teese cites her as an influence). The Marchesa saw things differently: Her goal, she announced, was to be "a living work of art." At her unfinished palazzo on the Grand Canal, she received everyone from **Picasso** to Man Ray, who immortalized his hostess in a famous triple-exposure of her hypnotic eyes. After the extravagances of the '20s, however, Casati was obliged to scale back her entertaining. She died in London and is buried in Brompton Cemetery, her taxidermied Pekingese at her feet.

WALLIS SIMPSON, DUCHESS OF WINDSOR
(1896–1986)

"Mine is a simple story. It is the story of an ordinary life that became extraordinary." That's how Wallis Simpson began her 1956 autobiography, *The Heart Has Its Reasons*. It's a rather artless way of covering some eyebrow-raising territory. Born out of wedlock and twice divorced, Wallis nevertheless married the king of England, who abdicated rather than give her up. Though it sounds very romantic, the Windsor marriage gives the impression of being quite dreary: Having landed her man, Wallis was then stuck with him. What fascinates designers is her much-vaunted neatness; her hair was so sleek, it was said, that a fly would slip off it. She dressed absolutely correctly at all times, in prim suits for day and something a little whimsical (often courtesy of **Schiaparelli**) by night. "I'm nothing to look at," she once remarked. "All I can do is dress better than anyone else."

MILLICENT ROGERS (1903–1953)

Any time you see a designer incorporate elements of the American Southwest into a collection, you can be sure Millicent Rogers was a source of inspiration. In the 1940s, two decades before hippies discovered the charm of silver-and-turquoise Navajo jewelry, she liked to mix it with her tailored suits and **Charles James** dresses, a then-unheard-of combination of high-fashion and ethnic costume. Though she was born to money and grew up in Manhattan, Rogers was a proto-hippie with a fondness for boho dress. Before her fascination with the Southwest, she lived in the Austrian Alps, where she launched a craze for traditional Tyrolean dirndl skirts and peasant blouses. But it was in New Mexico, where she designed jewelry inspired by native craftspeople and collected Pueblo art, that she was happiest. Her Taos house is now a museum dedicated to Native American art.

THE SWANS: GLORIA GUINNESS (1912-1980), BABE PALEY (1915-1978), SLIM KEITH (1918-1990), and C. Z. GUEST (1920-2003)

As anyone who's read "La Côte Basque" knows, it wasn't easy being a friend of **Truman Capote**'s. But when things were going well, he certainly knew how to flatter a girl. The quartet he referred to as the Swans were, he said, "extremely attractive, alert and au courant," with "qualities of style and appearance and amusing good sense beyond the point of easy youthful beguilement." Certainly legions of fashion designers have agreed with him—references to them are as perennial as little black dresses and pearls. Gloria Guinness, the most mysterious of the Swans, was a Mexican-born beauty who exemplified laid-back glamour. Her friend Babe Paley was a more refined version of Gloria, with the added self-assuredness of the impeccably ancestored. Slim Keith was the original California girl, and C.Z. was the personification of haute WASPness at its most tasteful. Taken together, they're a visual lexicon of American style.

EDIE SEDGWICK (1943-1971)

Poor Edie. She wanted to be an actress, but she was only ever a mess. Not that that's stopped anyone from copying her uniform of black tights and something abbreviated on top, a look Edie was supposedly able to carry off thanks to extensive massage to slim her legs. She had a brief success as a model in **Diana Vreeland**'s *Vogue* before taking up with **Andy Warhol** in 1965. That's when her spectacular self-implosion, fueled by alcohol, amphetamines, and, later, heroin and barbiturates, really got under way. She quickly became one of Warhol's Superstars, appearing in films such as *Chelsea Girls* (*Ciao Manhattan,* the quasi-biopic in which she plays a character named Susan Superstar, was directed by John Palmer and David Weisman). She then took up with Bob Dylan, who later immortalized her in "Just Like a Woman" ("her fog, her amphetamines, her pearls"). By 1971, she was dead of an overdose. Her most recent resurrection was in *Factory Girl* (2007), in which she was portrayed by Sienna Miller.

LIFESTYLE

According to *Webster's* dictionary, the word "lifestyle" was first used in 1939, to describe the "typical way of life of an individual, group, or culture." Presumably, before 1939 people had lives, not lifestyles. Which is to say they ate at home, wouldn't have recognized a celebrity chef if he'd showed up to cook Christmas dinner, and didn't go on holidays to exotic locales. They also didn't need books to tell them how to be cool. But life— or perhaps I should say lifestyle—has gotten a lot more cosmopolitan since then. Package tours and credit cards have made foreign travel and expensive restaurants commonplace, and magazines, cable television, and the Internet have rendered what one early example of voyeuristic programming called "the lifestyles of the rich and famous"—there's that word again—as familiar as your own daily routine. The challenge is to sort the wheat from the chaff. When anyone can buy a cheap ticket online, for example, the stakes for what makes a vacation spot recherché rise.

This chapter looks at what you need to know to distinguish yourself as a person of taste. From holiday destinations to chic hotels, impressive wines and uncommon cocktails, where to party now and where the beautiful people disgraced themselves before, it's here.

TEN PLACES TO GO ON HOLIDAY

WHERE YOU VACATION says as much about you as your shoes. The best jet-set resorts were popularized by hippies and retain their bohemian glamour even when the hotel charges require a platinum card. If you're striking out somewhere new, get there before the tour buses descend—they're a sure sign that the savvy travelers have moved on.

BRAZIL

Thanks to its reputation as a spawning ground for models, Brazil is enjoying a cultural renaissance that hasn't been matched since the heady days of bossa nova and Oscar Niemeyer. The newfound attention has resulted in a steady influx of tourists, all eager to partake of its exotic ambience and lazy, "Girl From Ipanema" sensuality.

It's Brazil's cities, in particular Rio de Janeiro and São Paulo, that have drawn the most attention. With Pão de Açúcar (Sugarloaf Mountain) rising up in the background and the Atlantic lapping at its edges, Rio has a spectacular natural setting, but it's the combination of year-round bikini weather and the enviable lifestyle of wealthier Cariocas, as the natives are called, that fascinates visitors from grayer, more sedate burgs. São Paulo, in the southeast, is Brazil's industrial heart, as well as its center of art (its Biennial is a major art fair), design, and fashion. It can't match Rio for looks, but Paulistas will inevitably tell you that theirs is the more sophisticated metropolis.

If beaches are your thing, Brazil has more than forty-six hundred miles of coastline—which is one reason it's being touted as the new Caribbean. The jet set head to the yachts and private villas of the 365 islands of Angra dos Reis on the Costa Verde southwest of Rio. Then there's Buzios, which was made famous in the 1960s by Brigitte Bardot. She's now considered its patron saint—there's even a life-size bronze statue of her on the main drag. Cariocas who find Buzios overdeveloped prefer Parati, with its beautiful Portuguese colonial architecture. Brazilian fashionistas, meanwhile, head for the difficult-to-reach (unless you have a private boat or helicopter) hamlet of Trancoso, in the northern state of Bahia. It still resembles the simple fishing village it once was, but ever since the manager of Daslu, an exclusive—i.e., the salesgirls are local socialites—boutique in São Paulo had a New Year's Eve bash here a few years ago, property prices in the area have been skyrocketing.

THE DALMATIAN COAST

Some holiday destinations are so storied that just to mention them is to conjure up images of rosy, carefree bliss. St.-Tropez. Ibiza. Tahiti. Who wouldn't want to go there? But there's a catch to all of these fantasies: They're rooted in the past. The St.-Tropez you really want to go to peaked in 1955, when Brigitte Bardot and Roger Vadim arrived to film *And God Created Woman*. Ibiza, meanwhile, was at its best in the 1960s and Tahiti in the '70s. Going to any of these places now means encountering high prices, long lines, and a sinking feeling that you've been had. If the thrill of discovery is the catalyst for travel, then in these cases, the thrill is gone.

To be able to tell "I was in [insert name of exotic locale] before [some mass tourism disaster]" stories requires a degree of intrepidness.

The place intrepid travelers are journeying to at the moment is the Dalmatian Coast in Croatia. It's not that the area's never had tourists but rather that they disappeared in 1991, when Yugoslavia's decade-long civil war started. Though Croatia was never as badly affected as Serbia and Bosnia, no one, quite understandably, wanted to be anywhere near there.

What makes the area such a draw is that it has a little of everything: The coastal landscape, with its craggy cliffs dropping down to sandy beaches that ring hundreds of tiny, private-feeling coves, is one of the most spectacular in Europe; the cities and towns, especially Dubrovnik and the island fortress of Korcula, are amazingly well preserved and relatively unspoiled; the pace of life is relaxed; the nightlife is sufficiently thumping (especially on the island of Hvar); the food is good; and the wine is very good (inland Istria, Croatia's wine country, is being promoted as the next Provence). All that's missing is five-star hotels, but by the time they arrive—and that won't be long—you'll be kicking yourself for not going sooner.

GOA, INDIA

Goa, a small state located midway down India's western flank, on the Arabian Sea, is not what most people expect when they think of India. For one thing, it's known for its beaches, not its crowded urban centers. And because it was once a Portuguese colony, it has something of a Mediterranean feel to it. Whitewashed churches and convents, clay-tiled roofs, and wrought-iron balconies are common architectural features (and best seen in Old Goa, now a UNESCO World Heritage site). The Portuguese were booted out in 1961, but they were soon replaced by a new variety of colonizer, one that traveled not by sailing ship but via VW bus overland from Europe: hippies. Like **Morocco**, Goa was once a thriving outpost of international hippiedom. Its capital was the village of Anjuna, formerly a sort of permanent Woodstock and now the site of a renowned flea market.

Though the VW buses have rolled on, Goa's reputation as a place where alternative lifestyles are welcome remains, and the flower children have been replaced by succeeding waves of alt-tour-ists, from the new agers of the '80s to the ravers of the '90s, who made Goa trance music a global phenomenon. The latest wave of refugees from everyday life to wash up on Goa's beaches are yoga devotees, many with ties to the fashion industry, who come to do warrior poses and salutations to the sun with top instructors. And then there are the people who just get to go on holiday a lot, like Kate Moss and Jade Jagger, both of whom have stayed at the harem-chic Nilaya Hermitage Hotel, which is run by a former Parisian fashion stylist.

But as with any destination that's been added to the flight routes of budget airlines, Goa's not quite the idyllic paradise it once was. Best avoided are the package-tour towns of Baga and Calangute, which are evolving into havens for the all-you-can-eat-buffet crowd.

THE GREEK ISLANDS

Long before Jacqueline Kennedy married Aristotle Onassis on Skorpios and took to spending her free time cruising around the Aegean Sea, the sun-soaked Greek Islands were drawing a well-heeled crowd. But Mrs. O's trendsetter reputation went a long way toward giving them a tourism boost: When she and Ari docked at Mykonos for the night, it was catapulted from backwater to glam-orous port of call almost as quickly (the paparazzi photo of her sunbathing in the nude on one of the islands had a similar effect on *Penthouse*'s sales, but that's another story).

The Cyclades Islands, which include Mykonos and Santorini, remain the best known of the Greek Islands—and the most expen-sive. With their whitewashed houses and dramatic vistas, they look tailor-made for a Calvin Klein ad, a factor that's clearly not lost on their fashionable visitors. Low-lying Mykonos is where to go if you want to indulge in all-out hedonism: Rising at noon, sun-ning all afternoon, and partying until dawn is a typical schedule here. It's also got a sizable gay scene at Paradise Beach, though that's not quite as wild as it once was. Far more sedate is the equally lovely Santorini, which is quiet enough to have a very thoughtful bookstore, Atlantis Books, in the village of Oia.

Less crowded are the Eptanissa Islands, on the other side of the Greek mainland, in the Ionian Sea. Unlike the stark Cyclades, the Ionians are lush and green—even the sugar-cube houses are draped with bougainvillea. And because they were ruled at various points by the Venetians, the French, and the British, they have a unique culture and architecture. Corfu, which is supposedly the island where Shakespeare shipwrecked Prospero, was the former summer headquarters of the Greek royal family. It gets the most tourists, though its beaches are a bit pebbly. Catching up fast is Kefalonia, where the runaway best seller *Captain Corelli's Mandolin* is set. But don't let that scare you off—it's lovely.

GSTAAD, SWITZERLAND

How important is skiing to the super-rich? Well, Le Rosey, the exclusive Swiss boarding school that charges tuition fees starting in the neighborhood of sixty-two thousand dollars a year and counts Julian Casablancas and Albert Hammond Jr. of the Strokes; actress Tracee Ellis Ross, daughter of Diana Ross; and a fair number of minor European royals amongst its alumni, feels strongly that all its graduates should be accomplished on the *piste*. Every winter, the entire school moves from its base in the Château du Rosey in the village of Rolle to a cluster of chalets in Gstaad, where students can benefit from some of the top ski instruction in the world.

Though it's less social than either St. Moritz or Zermatt, two of Switzerland's other top skiing destinations, Gstaad remains the quintessential winter resort of the elite (it should be noted, however, that the meaning of elite is more elastic than it used to be; Paris Hilton has made appearances here). Prince Rainer and Princess Grace owned a chalet in the village, and Kofi Annan, Roger Moore, and Ursula Andress have all been spotted on the slopes.

Until the mid-nineteenth century, most people visited the Alps in the summertime, when the genteel could indulge in sightseeing and the adventurous could go climbing. That changed in 1856, when a St. Moritz innkeeper by the name of Johannes Badrutt built the first-ever toboggan run and persuaded some English climbers to stay for the winter months. They had a fantastic time, went home and raved about it, and the winter resort was born. The concept really took off in the 1920s, when skiing, previously an obscure Scandinavian mode of travel, was adopted as a sport by the wealthy, the only people who had the money and time to spend on it. Gstaad, located in one of the snowiest cantons in Switzerland and already the home of several plush hotels, quickly became the place to be seen both *pendant* and après ski, a title it still holds today.

JOSÉ IGNACIO, URUGUAY

If there were a jet-set version of Where in the World Is Carmen Sandiego, the children's culture-and-geography trivia game, the title character would be Naomi Campbell. Whether she's ringing in the New Year in **St. Barts** or sunning herself on a yacht in the South of France, the peripatetic supermodel has an unparalleled knack for being where the champagne-fueled action is. Which is why when she's in South America, you'll find her in José Ignacio, a sophisticated resort masquerading as a rustic fishing village that is to **Buenos Aires** what the Hamptons are to New York City—i.e., a bucolic version of city life, complete with fantastic restaurants, plenty of nightlife, and an agreeably quiet stretch of sand on which to show off a Missoni bikini. In January and February, the height of the South American summer, it's the preferred holiday spot for wealthy Argentineans and their internationally fabulous friends, a group that includes, along with Ms. Campbell, **Mario Testino**, who's used the beach for fashion shoots, and hotelier Alan Faena, owner of **Buenos Aires**'s **Faena Hotel + Universe**.

The town is situated on a peninsula in the northeast quadrant of Uruguay, between the Atlantic Ocean and the Río de la Plata, a convenient half-hour flight from B.A. It's not far from Punta del Este, another resort town, but one that's not quite as esteemed as it was in the 1960s, when it was known as the Pearl of the Atlantic and attracted a steady flow of film stars, shipping magnates, and wealthy playboys. Multiple concrete hotels and tacky nightclubs later, it's slid down the social scale, a fate eco-conscious José is determined to avoid. Though international chains are eyeing it, so far the idyllic appeal of its sheltered beach, dirt roads, and groves of fragrant eucalyptus and pine trees has been spared any heavy-handed development.

MOROCCO

In the 1960s, Morocco was one of the essential stops on the hippie trail—Crosby, Stills & Nash even included a song about it, "Marrakesh Express," on their 1969 debut album. That same year, photographer Patrick Lichfield snapped one of the decade's most fabled images, of a caftan-wearing Talitha Getty and her husband, oil heir John Paul Getty, lounging druggily on the roof of their house in Marrakesh. Between the tune-in, turn-on CSN crowd and the boho-chic revelers who flew in from London (where the Gettys lived) and Paris, the counterculture tourists of the '60s gave this North African country a reputation as a place to pursue exotic, vaguely decadent leisure amid *Arabian Nights* architecture and boundless sunshine.

The hippies, both the barefoot and the expensively shod varieties, clustered around Marrakech, in the foothills of the Atlas Mountains. Morocco's biggest city is still the best equipped to deal with tourists—the narrow, winding streets of the medieval medina are filled with *riads* (traditional Moroccan houses) that have been extravagantly renovated into boutique hotels, trendy bars and restaurants, and stylish art galleries and boutiques. **Yves Saint Laurent** owns a *riad* here, as does Jean Paul Gaultier, and it's where you're most likely to spot celebrities, especially during the international film festival, when the city's famous central square, Place Jemaa el-Fna, becomes a giant outdoor cinema. Tangier, in the north, is more like a North African version of St.-Tropez, a working port that's rapidly evolving into a cosmopolitan resort. Casablanca is known for its pristine **art deco** architecture, while Fez, the religious and cultural capital of the country, is one of the most perfectly preserved medieval cities in the world. But the country's best-kept secret is Essaouira, the beach town that inspired Jimi Hendrix's "Castles in the Sand." Laid-back and still relatively undeveloped, it's where hip Marrakeshis escape to when the weekend influx of Europeans becomes too much.

PUGLIA, ITALY

A good general rule of thumb when traveling is to go where a country's natives go. In Italy, that's Puglia. Italians don't go to Tuscany or Umbria or Capri, or any other place that's been invaded by guidebook-clutching foreigners—they're far too relaxed to contemplate that sort of stress. Instead, they head for the heel of the Italian boot, a rocky peninsula that juts out into the Adriatic Sea to the west and the Ionian Sea to the east. What you'll find there is pretty much what you'll find in the rest of Italy, which is to say glorious scenery, rustic charm, pretty beaches, and—especially—fantastic food. That's a given everywhere in this food-obsessed country, but Puglia supplies a large percentage of Italy's pasta, olive oil, and fish, so eating here means feasting at the source. Furthermore, Puglia's muscular, full-flavored cuisine has yet to be interpreted by restaurants from Miami to Tokyo, which means that each meal offers an opportunity to savor something new. What you won't find in Puglia are hordes of people or that theme-park feeling that everything's been prepackaged for your safe and predictable enjoyment. And the stark white buildings of the villages, unusual for Italy and a complete contrast to the baroque fantasies found in the region's larger towns, are a reminder of just how close North Africa is.

The best option for lodging here is one of the converted *masseria* (fortified farmhouses) that dot the landscape. Again, these are unusual in Italy, a rocky country without much arable land, which means that farmers tend to live in town and commute to their fields. That newly renovated *masserias* are popping up with clockwork regularity is a sure sign that Puglia is on the verge of being Tuscanified.

RIVIERA MAYA, MEXICO

With its strip of bland high-rise hotels, bands of beer-chugging students, and *Girls Gone Wild* camera crews roaming in search of fresh talent, Cancún is exactly the sort of place you *don't* want to go on holiday. But the Yucatán Peninsula is not all garishness. Just a few miles south of Cancún's dubious charms stretches a 230-mile ribbon of white sand and turquoise water fringed with palm trees and known as the Riviera Maya. Thirty years ago, when it was known as the Costa Maya, there wasn't even a hotel here. In the intervening three decades, the area has been reinvented as the Caribbean's answer to the Côte d'Azur, and its newly opened boutique hotels and environmentally friendly resorts, where renewable energy sources and locally sourced building materials and foods are standard, are the last word in eco chic.

It's truly an astonishingly beautiful part of the world. The beaches, with their powdery quartz sand and rolling surf protected by a coral reef that's second in size only to Australia's Great Barrier Reef, are postcard gorgeous, and the clear blue-green water attracts divers from all over the world. If you want to break the languid pace of beach, food, and sleep with some culture, you can: Beyond the sands and palm trees are some of the best-preserved Mayan ruins in Mexico.

The farther away you get from the glare of Cancún, the less conventionally luxurious the accommodations get. Maroma, built by a hippie architect who arrived here in the early '60s, is the resort that kicked off the Riviera Maya phenomenon. Once fairly bare-bones, it's now plush enough to attract British royals. The determinedly bohemian, however, head for Tulum, where you can stay in thatch-roofed cabanas within a stone's throw of the surf, take yoga classes on the sand (yoga is *big* in Tulum), and catch up on your rest—the nightlife is minimal, and many of the hotels have no electricity after 9 P.M.

ST. BARTS

If you are even an occasional reader of glossy magazines, you know that St. Barts in the French West Indies is the kind of place where people stand around on yachts talking about how much money they've made from their (a) clothing line, (b) latest film, or (c) stock options. A private boat is actually the best way to arrive at St. Barts, a compact (it measures only eight square miles) isle that's too small and mountainous to handle any plane bigger then a puddle-jumper. The short runway is on the beach, and even experienced island-hoppers find the landing nerve-wracking: Pilots, who need a special license to attempt it, must first maneuver between two sharp peaks, then drop suddenly and steeply to the ground.

But then inaccessibility is part of what gives St.-Barthélemy its exclusive allure. It's also incredibly expensive—even in the off-season hotel tariffs range from the high- to mid-three figures a night, and there's even no such thing as a cheap lunch anywhere on the island. Most people, however, stay in fully staffed rented villas. And the off-season is most of the year, because the only time that really matters on St. Barts is the two-week period around Christmas and New Year's, when models and movie stars are as common as the immaculately groomed sand that passes for dirt here. The rest of the year, most of St. Barts' tourists are everyday rich, as opposed to obscenely rich, French people, a legacy of the island's status as a French colony that was first settled in the seventeenth century. Its standing as a playground for the wealthy, however, is relatively new. Up until about thirty-five years ago, this rocky, arid island was one of the poorest in the Caribbean. It was only when people with names like Rothschild and Rockefeller started dropping by that it developed into a little corner of the French Riviera in the New World.

FIVE CITIES
TO VISIT NOW

WITH THE ADVENT of the low-cost airline, the concept of the far-flung city break has arrived. For those times when you don't have the two weeks for a proper vacation but want a change of scene, these are the places to go.

BEIJING

If your image of Beijing is that of a city full of Mao-suited cyclists, you're behind the times. Black Audis have replaced bikes, and designer clothes, either real or counterfeit, are the preferred garb. The Chinese capital is in the midst of a building frenzy that was pushed into overdrive when it was announced that it would host the 2008 summer Olympics, with world-class talents like **Rem Koolhaas** and Herzog & de Meuron all putting their mark on the city. But architecture's not the only reason to visit—as China emerges from behind the scrim of Communism, Beijing is its most vibrant city, pulsating with entrepreneurial moxie. Its Factory 798 district is the center of the much ballyhooed Chinese art world (though Shanghai is coming up fast), the

PRONUNCIATION GUIDE

Houhai:
ho-HIGH

alleyways near Houhai, north of the Forbidden City, are home to dozens of bars and restaurants, and from its antiques markets to its newly opened luxury boutiques, it's a burgeoning consumer paradise.

BERLIN

To some, Berlin's moment of cool peaked when fashion designer Hedi Slimane turned up a few years ago, camera and sketchbook in hand. By the time he'd translated the skinny silhouettes he saw there into his Dior Homme collection, pundits would have it, the city's much-vaunted zeitgeist had melted into mainstream mush. While there's no denying the secret's out, Berlin is still drawing a savvy international crowd. In some ways, it's like New York in the '80s: graffiti proliferates, cheap rents are fueling an art boom, and the decadent nightlife, a tradition that dates back at least as far as Marlene Dietrich in her *Blue Angel* days, is more risqué than ever. The art scene is centered around the rapidly gentrifying Mitte

PRONUNCIATION GUIDE

Mitte:
mi-TUH

neighborhood in the former East Berlin, where the population's stay-up-late, get-up-late lifestyle means there are both lots of clubs and lots of cafés to get caffeinated in. If you need a more highbrow excuse to visit, Berlin has some great architecture, including one of **Le Corbusier**'s Unité d'Habitation housing developments.

BUENOS AIRES

Though calling Buenos Aires the Paris of South America is a cliché, like all clichés, it's rooted in truth: With its wide boulevards, stately beaux arts town houses, and leafy parks, the Argentine capital looks more Euro than Rio. But, like bleach-blond Eva Perón in her **Dior** suits, it's got an exuberant spirit beneath the carefully tasteful facade—this is, after all, the place where the tango was invented. Evita's tomb, in Recoleta Cemetery, Argentina's most recherché afterlife address, still draws legions of fans, but for a taste of B.A.'s style renaissance, Palermo Viejo (which is further subdivided into the Palermos Soho, Hollywood, and, er, Queens) is the place to go. Rather than looking to Europe, as their parents and grandparents did, the city's current generation of entrepreneurs have turned this former working-class neighborhood into ground zero for contemporary Argentine dining, design, and fashion. The other factor driving interest in B.A. is Argentina's stumbling economy: Thanks to the devalued peso, everything from a five-course meal at a top restaurant to antiques from the San Telmo flea market in the city's oldest quarter can be had for next to nothing.

ISTANBUL

Ever since the nineteenth century, when it was still known as Constantinople, literary travelers like Lord Byron and **Gustave Flaubert** have been inspired by Istanbul. And well into the twentieth century, it was perceived as the gateway to the mysterious Orient, a dream city of veiled harems and raucous bazaars. The harems are gone and the bazaars now sell bootleg DVDs, but the buzz surrounding twenty-first-century Istanbul reflects this long-held fascination, now given a fresh relevance: As the bridge between Europe and Asia (literally—the city straddles the Bosporus River, which divides the two continents), it's on the front line of the meeting of Western secularism and Islam, a factor that's been causing some consternation since Turkey began campaigning to join the European Union. But its appeal goes beyond its unique cultural heritage. Thanks to events like Istanbul Design Week and the Istanbul Biennial, the city whose ancient skyline encompasses Ottoman minarets, Christian steeples, and modernist skyscrapers is emerging as a capital of art and design.

MONTREAL

Predominantly French-speaking Montreal has always been something of an anomaly in North America, which is precisely what makes it worth visiting—it's not like any other city on the continent. Founded by the French in 1642, then taken over by the British in 1759, it was at the center of the Québécois separatist movement of the 1970s and '80s. But the rancor has died down as the economy has blossomed, and Montrealers have by and large gotten back to what they do best: eating, drinking, and generally having a good time. Old Montreal, also known as Vieux-Montréal, with its gray limestone buildings and cobblestone streets, is now home to plush boutique hotels and hip restaurants, while the more bohemian Plateau Mont Royal is a world-class shopping and clubbing neighborhood. The city hosts jazz, comedy, and film festivals in the summertime, but to really get a sense of what it's like to maintain joie de vivre in the face of subzero temperatures, visit in the winter months.

THE TEN
CHICEST HOTELS
IN THE WORLD

STAYING AT ANY of these hotels is like living a grown-up Eloise-at-the-Plaza fantasy, only more glamorous. Some are legendary for their history, others for their decor or amenities; all guarantee a memorable stay.

THE CHATEAU MARMONT, LOS ANGELES

Before André Balazs took it over in 1991, the Chateau Marmont was remembered primarily as the place where John Belushi died of a drug overdose. But even if the hotel's heyday had been momentarily eclipsed, it had had a long and glamorous past as the scene of some of Hollywood's most spectacular triumphs and debaucheries. The Chateau was where **F. Scott Fitzgerald** wrote his unfinished final novel, *The Last Tycoon*. It's where **Roman Polanski** hid out before skipping the country to avoid statutory rape charges, where Greta Garbo went to be alone, where **Dorothy Parker** lived and

PRONUNCIATION GUIDE
André Balazs:
ahn-DRAY ba-LASH

drank with her much younger husband, where June and **Helmut Newton** spent the winter, and where Led Zeppelin raced Harley-Davidsons down the corridors. It's the Hotel California that the Eagles sang about, where you can check out, but you can never leave. In a city of constant sunshine, the Chateau is a dark oasis in which anything goes, and that's just the way its loyal guests like it.

By the time Balazs bought it, however, all these antics had taken a toll on the Loire Valley–style building, which opened in 1929 as an apartment complex. But rather than getting rid of everything that people loved about the old Marmont, Balazs just tidied it up: The hotel's suites, bungalows, and public spaces have retained the low-key Old Hollywood glamour that the place is steeped in. The rooms are furnished with old lamps, Noguchi-style coffee tables, bark-cloth curtains, and boxy sofas. Even the bathrooms are lovingly restored versions of the 1930s originals. It doesn't feel designed, but rather lived in by someone who's too glamorous to care about modernizing—wandering into the Gothic salon feels like dropping in on Norma Desmond in *Sunset Boulevard* (which was also written here). And because the restaurant is tiny and the only bar is in a separate building, it has the feeling of an exclusive club—one where the staff would never be indiscreet about the behavior of the members.

CLARIDGE'S, LONDON

It's hard to choose just one highlight from Claridge's long history. The Great Exhibition of 1851, when it was the preferred pied à terre for European nobles who made the trek to London to see wonders such as the glass-and-wrought-iron Crystal Palace? The time Queen Victoria and Prince Albert arrived to take tea with Empress Eugènie of France, who'd made the hotel her headquarters for the winter of 1860? Or the 1945 birth of the heir to the throne of Yugoslavia, for which Prime Minister Winston Churchill declared his parents' suite Yugoslav territory? Even today, when arguably more luxurious hotels have sprung up in the British capital, Claridge's remains the choice for those who appreciate tradition.

The current building dates from 1898, but Claridge's roots go back to 1812, when James Mivart opened a hotel in well-to-do

Mayfair, still the neighborhood to visit if you want to buy a complete shooting kit or toothpaste from the people who supply Buckingham Palace. In 1854 Mivart sold his business to William and Marianne Claridge, who gave the hotel its present name and made it synonymous with the best of everything. It was under their direction that Claridge's became a fixture in aristocratic life—even the British royal family, who certainly have plenty of options to choose from, occasionally have private parties here.

Like England's grand houses, Claridge's doesn't go in for frequent overhauls. Its last major makeover occurred in 1996, and that was the first since the 1930s. Consequently, its mix of **art deco** and classic English country-house decor can seem a bit shabby around the edges, but that's part of its charm. Taking tea in the lobby, which has been a tradition since the turn of the last century, or dining at **Gordon Ramsay**'s restaurant here has a special-treat quality—you feel that you should be on your best behavior when you walk into Claridge's.

HÔTEL COSTES, PARIS

With its heavy Second Empire furniture, swagged and tasseled red-velvet drapes, leopard prints, and brass-potted ferns—all courtesy of maximalist designer Jacques Garcia—the Hôtel Costes feels like an especially opulent belle-epoque brothel. But while the references are archly Old World, the attitude is pure twenty-first-century fashion hothouse: From the patrons (photographers, editors, Charlotte Gainsbourg, Catherine Deneuve) to the music played at the bar (resident DJ Stéphane Pompougnac has so far released nine compilations of signature Costes chill-out tunes), there is no more style-conscious hotel in the world than the Costes. Even the notoriously capricious **Yves Saint Laurent** has given it his stamp of approval by lunching there twice a week.

The hotel is the brainchild of brothers Jean-Louis and Gilbert Costes, Paris's trendsetting *limonadiers,* or café owners. The Costes brothers burst onto the scene in 1983, with the **Philippe Starck** designed Café Costes in Les Halles, the interior of which was inspired by Budapest's Keleti Railway Station. Their design credentials established, the brothers rapidly expanded their empire to include some of the city's chicest and most shrewdly marketed dining spots, including the Georges, the stylish canteen atop the **Centre Georges Pompidou**, the Café Marly at the Louvre, which overlooks **I. M. Pei**'s glass **Pyramid**, and l'Esplanade, the only café on the grand Esplanade des Invalides. But it's the Costes, a former late-nineteenth-century town house they transformed into a hotel in 1995, that is the shining crown jewel in their empire of hip.

In a city brimming with pedigreed hotels and deluxe rooms, the secret of the Costes's success lies in its attitude to celebrity: If you're famous in a slightly louche or even camp way, the Costes will coddle you like an infant in a nursery (which is perhaps why Johnny Depp reportedly calls the concierge Papa). For everyone else, the lure lies in pretending, just for a few days, to be part of all this fabulousness.

HÔTEL DU CAP EDEN-ROC, ANTIBES, FRANCE

In 1863, when a group of Russian aristocrats built Villa Soleil, the French Riviera was a winter resort, more or less deserted after April, when the wealthy English families who were its main patrons gathered up their parasols and steamer rugs and headed north. It remained so until 1923, when the villa, which had been reinvented as the Hôtel du Cap in 1870, was rented out for the summer by an expat American couple named Sara and Gerald Murphy. They invited their glamorous friends, including **Picasso** and the **F. Scott Fitzgerald**s to visit them, threw a few parties, and, suddenly, the Riviera in high summer became the place to be. Fitzgerald was so taken with the Hôtel du Cap that he made it the model for the Hôtel des Etrangers (and his hosts the models for his two main characters) in *Tender Is the Night.*

The creamy white villa, set in acres of manicured gardens and fresh-smelling pine forest midway between Nice and Cannes, still has the feel of the private-members club it once was. You can stay either in the main building, where the cool white bedrooms, decorated in a mix of French antiques and overstuffed cream sofas, are accessed via an antique lift; in one of two additional wings; or in one of two private villas. Meals are taken on a two-level terrace that overlooks the sea. Though Fitzgerald gave the hotel a "bright tan prayer rug of a beach," this part of the Côte d'Azur is actually quite rocky. However, there is a saltwater pool for guests to swim in. During the Cannes film festival, it's a good place to spot the many celebrities who make the Hôtel du Cap their temporary headquarters. But even for them, the hotel doesn't break its one inflexible rule: It doesn't accept credit cards. If you want to stay at the Hôtel du Cap, be prepared to arrive with a suitcase full of cash or a draft from your banker.

FAENA HOTEL + UNIVERSE, BUENOS AIRES

There's a time for understated Old World luxury, and there's a time for completely self-indulgent, ultra-opulent, bordering-on-the-lurid extravagance, the kind that makes you think that Gianni Versace must be exercising his ghostly influence from the big runway in the sky.

PRONUNCIATION GUIDE
Faena:
FAH-na

When the latter is called for, it's time to head for the Faena, a **Buenos Aires** hotel that's not just a place to sleep but an entire universe. It was dreamed up by the celebrity Argentine property developer Alan Faena, who's a sort of white-clad, cowboy-hat-wearing Donald Trump of the Pampas. Looking at B.A.'s once bustling old port area, Puerto Madero, he decided that it was prime real estate in need of just a few extravagant tweaks to make it bustle once again. The first part of his grand plan is the 108-room Faena Hotel + Universe, housed in a cavernous former grain warehouse that was done up by the ubiquitous **Philippe Starck** (who's called it "the best creation I've ever done") in a bloodred and snow-white color scheme that mixes high kitsch (plaster unicorn heads) with a winking interpretation of traditional luxuries (the guest rooms' state-of-the-art sound systems are mounted on revolving platforms).

As its name suggests, the Faena's purview is wide-ranging. Once you've entered the hotel via its nave-like lobby, there are plenty of excuses to stay, including two restaurants, a gym, a pool, a hammam, a library, and a performance space (the last is part of Faena's scheme to turn Puerto Madero into B.A.'s next arts center). If you exhaust those possibilities, you can always get one of the hotel's friendly "experience managers" to organize tango lessons, tickets to a polo match, or treks to Patagonia for you.

The Faena's high glitz factor may not appeal to all tastes, but for urban nomads in search of fresh stimulation, it's a great big bowl of candy.

FOUR SEASONS ISTANBUL, ISTANBUL

Remember Billy Hayes, the hapless young American who was thrown into a hellish Turkish jail for drug smuggling in the 1978 film *Midnight Express*? Well, Billy wouldn't recognize his old digs now: The century-old prison where he was sentenced to spend thirty years has been transformed into the ultraluxurious Four Seasons Istanbul (to continue with the rehabilitated-drug-scene lore for a moment, you can also stay in the late Colombian drug kingpin Pablo Escobar's former beach house in Tulum, which, in an equally bizarre twist of fate, has been turned into a resort). The Turkish neoclassical building was designated a national treasure in honor of the numerous writers, artists, and scholars who were incarcerated there during Turkey's dark days of political repression, so the bright yellow exterior has been left largely as it originally was. Inside, glass additions link the series of high-ceilinged, large-windowed buildings that frame the open courtyard, which is paved with Ottoman tiles and filled with greenery. The sixty-five rooms and suites, meanwhile, have been individually decked out with new and antique Turkish furniture, kilims, artwork, and artifacts.

Because it's in the oldest part of Istanbul, the hotel is within walking distance of many of the city's most famous sites, a list that includes such impressive haunts as Topkapi Palace (scene of the 1964 heist caper *Topkapi*); Hagia Sophia, the sixth-century domed Eastern Orthodox church-turned-mosque-turned-museum that's considered one of the most impressive buildings ever erected; the breathtaking Blue Mosque; the fanciful nineteenth-century Beylerbeyi Palace, where visiting dignitaries like the Duke and **Duchess of Windsor** used to be put up; and Sirkeci Station, onetime southern terminal of the fabled Orient Express. Connected to the station is the Petra Palace Hotel, once the finest in Istanbul, where Agatha

Christie holed up in 1933 to write *Murder on the Orient Express*. Take a stroll near the Four Seasons, or just look out at the city from one of its rooftop terraces, and you'll understand why she extended her stay.

THE MERCER, NEW YORK CITY

If you've ever fantasized about living in a loft in Manhattan's SoHo neighborhood, the Mercer, a former fur warehouse built for John Jacob Astor II in 1890, is the place to test-drive your dream. Each of its seventy-five rooms was designed to feel like the idealized lofts that non–New Yorkers imagine are found on every block in Gotham, with high ceilings, acres of unfettered space, huge windows, and a spotless white decor. No one in New York really lives this way, but that's part of the Mercer's charm—it's a more comfortable version of urban life than the one that exists outside its doors, complete with oversize bath-tubs topped with skylights and twenty-four-hour room service from **Jean-Georges Vongerichten**'s Mercer Kitchen in the basement.

PRONUNCIATION GUIDE

**Jean-Georges Vongerichten:
ZHAHN-zhorzh
vong-uh-RICK-ten**

The hotel was opened in 1997 by **André Balazs**, who also owns the **Chateau Marmont**. Like the Chateau, the Mercer is a celebrity favorite—if the hotel's name sounds familiar, it's probably because practically every actor or rock star interview published since it opened has taken place in its lobby. But don't expect to hang out in the lobby and gawk; it's for guests only. If you're just coming in off the street, you'll be politely directed to the adjoining café, which overlooks the corner of Mercer and Prince streets, a great spot to observe the blend of new, shopping-driven SoHo (the hotel is conveniently located between the Prada and Apple shops) and old, arty SoHo, exemplified by Fanelli's, the dark, century-plus-old bar across the street.

As conceived by Paris-based Christian Liaigre, who's decked the hotel out with his signature African Wenge wood furniture, neutral textiles, and dark wood floors, the Mercer is understatedly luxurious. It was designed for people who are constantly on the move but don't want to be reminded they're in a hotel. There are no conference facilities, no tour groups, and no business center, just chic comfort.

PARK HYATT TOKYO, TOKYO

Though it didn't get equal billing with Bill Murray or Scarlett Johansson, Tokyo's Park Hyatt, where the pair conducts much of their jet-lagged quasi-courtship, is arguably the star of Sofia Coppola's *Lost in Translation*. In fact, Coppola has said that before she was certain what shape the film would take, she knew she wanted to set it in Tokyo at the Park Hyatt, which she's described as "one of my favorite places in the world."

It's easy to understand the director's fondness for the hotel. For bleary-eyed travelers arriving from the West, the Park Hyatt is a sort of crash-course in the beautiful strangeness of contemporary Japanese culture. It's perched on the top fourteen floors of the fifty-two-story Shinjuku Park Tower, a trio of glass-and-granite buildings designed by Kenzo Tange, the Pritzker Prize–winning father of modern Japanese architecture (he redesigned Hiroshima after the atomic bombing). Though any of the hotel's windows offer a great view, the top-floor gym is the best place to take in both Tokyo's vast neon sprawl and the timeless serenity of Mount Fuji. Add the Zen-inspired decor; the top-rated French restaurant, the Girandole; the New York Bar and Grill, with its enormous paintings of Big Apple scenes; and the traditional English tea served in the serene forty-first-floor bamboo garden, and you've got a uniquely Japanese take on embrace-it-all multiculturalism. No wonder Murray and Johansson wander around in such a daze.

The hotel has only 177 rooms, which is small by Asian standards. But each one of them is comparatively large and offers a traditional deep bath for soaking away the stress of travel. As you sink into the water, perhaps contemplating the extra-wide bed, it's hard to believe that you're in the center of one of the most hectic cities in the world.

PRINCIPE DI SAVOIA, MILAN

Most hotels lavish attention on their public rooms—lobbies, restaurants—and skimp on the bedrooms. So while your fantasy of staying in a Turkish pasha's palace or an English country house may hold up while you're having a drink at the bar, it wavers when it comes time to turn in. Not so at the Principe di Savoia, where the mood of over-the-top, Old World Italian grandeur never fades (it's especially

> **PRONUNCIATION GUIDE**
>
> **Principe di Savoia:
> preen-CHI-pay dee
> sa-VOY-ah**

prominent in the Presidential Suite, where the private pool is modeled after a Pompeiian bath and the bed is made up with cashmere sheets). Built in the 1920s and named for the last royal house to rule Italy, the Principe is pure theatrics all the way. Though there is a newer wing, the original building is the place to stay: The rooms have huge mirrors, embossed leather–covered doors, curtains that sink into brocade puddles on the floor, the kind of solid wardrobes that were built to hold bustled evening gowns, and black-and-white marble bathrooms. When you're here, it's possible to imagine that you're a character in a prewar novel, breaking your train journey in Milan.

But it's in the hotel's lobby bar, the Giardino d'Inverno, that the role-playing possibilities are best appreciated. The marble-lined room, topped with an enormous stained-glass dome, is furnished with damask arm chairs and loveseats grouped around small round tables,

> **PRONUNCIATION GUIDE**
>
> **Giardino d'Inverno:
> jahr-DEE-noh deen-VER-noh**

and you can order afternoon tea or cocktails from the white-jacketed waiters. The mood of old-fashioned, genteel formality is broken only by the jeans-wearing guests.

The Principe is a favorite of the younger fashion crowd, and during the Milan collections it overflows with magazine staff, buyers, and the many stylish hangers-on that fashion attracts, all of whom seem to sail into the lobby carrying designer shopping bags. In their own way, they're part of the decor.

HÔTEL RITZ, PARIS

Located smack in the middle of the elegant 1st arrondissement, just around the corner from some of the best shopping in the world (including Colette), the Ritz has been a part of Paris life since 1898, when César Ritz arrived in the French capital and turned the former *hôtel particulier* of the Duc de Lauzon into one of the world's first luxury hotels. Since then it's been a temporary home to everyone from the Duke and **Duchess of Windsor** to Winston Churchill to Donatella Versace. It was the primary residence of **Coco Chanel**, whose couture house is just across the street on the rue Cambon, from 1934 until her death in 1971, and where Marcel Proust spent most of his time when he wasn't scratching away in his cork-lined bedroom—he even immortalized Olivier Descade, the maître d'hôtel, in *A la recherche du temps perdu*.

But Proust is just one of the literary figures who've been associated with the Ritz. **Oscar Wilde** and **Truman Capote** stayed there, and **F. Scott Fitzgerald**, **Jean-Paul Sartre**, and **Simone de Beauvoir** drank at the bar. The Bloody Mary was invented there for Ernest Hemingway, who later gave his name to the hotel's Hemingway Bar (the Ritz's other bar is the Vendôme; both are favored local watering holes).

What's made the Ritz such an institution is its legendary service, instituted by the far-seeing Monsieur Ritz, whose motto was "I know what clients want today, but what will they want tomorrow?" (Modern conveniences, for one thing—the Ritz was the first hotel to have electricity, bathrooms, and telephones in each room.) He was also astute enough to hire the foremost chef of the day, Auguste Escoffier, whose high standards of French cuisine are maintained by Michel Roth at the hotel's L'Espadon restaurant. And then there's the unparalleled discretion and courtesy with which the staff of six hundred look after the 162 rooms. As Hemingway said, "When in Paris the only reason not to stay at the Ritz is if you can't afford it."

FIVE LEGENDARY NIGHTCLUBS OF THE PAST

WHETHER THE FASHION WAS for dinner and dancing or pills and performance art, these were the twentieth century's prime places to be seen when the sun went down.

ANNABEL'S, LONDON

As London started to swing in 1963, former adman Mark Birley recognized that the British aristocracy needed a place of their own to party. His response was to open a members-only club in a basement in Mayfair, London's poshest neighborhood, and name it after his wife, Lady Annabel, who's now best known as the mother of English-It-Girl/British-*Vogue*-party-pages-regular Jemima Kahn. Annabel's was an instant success: Lee Radziwill, Princess Margaret, and Aristotle Onassis all twisted and fugged their way around its minute dance floor in the '60s. Though the royals still show up—this is where Diana and Fergie crashed Prince Andrew's stag night dressed as policewomen—it's been distinctly less fabulous of late, especially since Birley and his son began feuding over ownership. Not long ago, one British newspaper described it as "the sort of place that the young avoided, in case they caught their father there with his mistress."

THE MUDD CLUB, NEW YORK

If the midtown **Studio 54** was where mainstream celebrities went to party, then the downtown Mudd Club, supposedly christened for the doctor who treated John Wilkes Booth (and subsequently became a social pariah) after he assassinated Abraham Lincoln, was where their counterculture counterparts gathered. Opened on Halloween 1978, in a loft in the then-no-man's-land of TriBeCa by publisher Steve Mass, artist Diego Cortez, and singer Anya Philips of the band the Contortions, the Mudd Club was a linchpin of New York's post-**punk/new wave** scene. The Ramones, **Blondie**, and Lydia Lunch all performed there, to crowds that included **Jean-Michel Basquiat**, **Nan Goldin**, and **Stephen Sprouse**. The club's unisex bathrooms were famous, as were its art gallery and its themed parties. Though influential, the Mudd

Mudd Club regular Debbie Harry shows off the mix of offhand glamour and new wave cool that made her one of the stars of the downtown New York scene.

Club was short-lived. Drugs and AIDS took their toll on the underground scene, and by the early '80s competing clubs had latched onto the mix of art and music that the Mudd Club originated.

RÉGINE'S, PARIS

Long before celebrities partied all night at **Studio 54**, there was Régine's, named for its single-monikered, flame-haired proprietor, a former Parisian hat-check girl who transformed herself into the Queen of the Night. The original discotheque—it was the first club to play recorded rather than live music and sell alcohol by the bottle—opened its doors in Paris in 1958 and eventually expanded into a worldwide chain, with branches in New York, St.-Tropez, London, São Paulo, and Rio. From the 1960s to the mid-'70s, Régine's was at the top of the nightlife pyramid, attracting everyone from **Andy Warhol** to Aristotle Onassis. High-flying regulars carried gold membership cards in Cartier holders; everyone else had to queue up and pass the peephole test. Régine's reign ended in the late '70s, when the fabulous started deserting her in scores for the more decadent pleasures of Studio 54.

THE STORK CLUB, NEW YORK

If any one place could claim to have spawned modern celebrity culture, it's the Stork Club. Founded in 1929 as a speakeasy by Sherman Billingsley, a Damon Runyon–esque bootlegger from Oklahoma, the Stork Club was America's most glamorous canteen in the 1930s and '40s, attracting debutantes, gangsters, actresses, sports stars, and politicians. Once past the solid-gold chain that kept out the riffraff, regulars such as Rita Hayworth, Frank Sinatra, and the Kennedys danced and dined on haute WASP specialties like chicken hash while Walter Winchell, the most powerful gossip columnist in the world, took notes for his syndicated column. Billingsley's genius for manipulating this now-familiar mix of exclusivity and media access made his club a byword for glamour, but by the late 1950s, he was struggling to attract the kind of patrons who once flocked to his door. The club closed in 1965.

STUDIO 54, NEW YORK

It's easy to toss around words like "legendary," but in the case of Studio 54, it's apt. From the man-in-the-moon with the animated cocaine spoon that hung over the dance floor to the shirtless bartenders, Studio 54 has become part of the culture, endlessly referenced and mourned. It was opened in 1977 by Steve Rubell and Ian Schrager (who went on to become an influential hotelier) and was named after its address on West Fifty-fourth Street in Manhattan. A democratic, quaalude-fueled hedonism was the order of the night: People like Bianca Jagger, who once rode into the club on a white horse for her birthday party, **Halston**, and **Diana Vreeland** mixed with "beautiful nobodies" Rubell handpicked from the crowds outside. The party ended in 1980, after Rubell and Schrager were arrested for skimming the club's profits. Studio 54 reopened again for a few years in the mid-'80s, but by then, the days of disco were over.

THE TEN MOST STYLISH RESTAURANTS IN THE WORLD

FROM THE FASHION SET'S FAVORITE to the Michelin-anointed, these establishments meet the three criteria that make a restaurant forever cool: good food, reliable service, and a low-key but self-assured ambience.

L'ATELIER DE JOËL ROBUCHON, PARIS

When he retired in 1995 at the age of fifty, Joël Robuchon was at the top of his game. **Alain Ducasse** might have amassed more Michelin stars, but it was Robuchon who was considered by his peers to be the most influential French chef of his generation—some said of the entire twentieth century. A lifetime in chef's whites didn't lead to a quiet retirement spent writing his memoirs, however. A few years after quitting the fast-paced world of haute cuisine, he was back, with a more low-key concept, a brasserie-cum-sushi-bar concept that concentrated on artisanal food made from scratch in an open kitchen—as the name suggests, more of a workshop than the hierarchical kitchens he'd made his name in. The idea was that patrons would sit around a bar sipping wine while watching the chefs do their thing. The first Atelier opened in Tokyo in 2001 and was followed by the Paris branch two years later. New York, Las Vegas, and London soon had their own outposts of this now international brand, but to those who make going to fashionable restaurants a way of life, the quintessential Atelier remains the Parisian one.

With its jars of vegetables and dangling hams (because Robuchon got the idea for the Ateliers in Spain, they always serve Iberian ham), it looks somewhat like a high-end grocer's, but is in fact a gastronomic French snack bar, where you can sample the recipes of a master chef in relatively unpretentious surroundings and for relatively low prices—the emphasis in both these cases being on the relative. The only seating is at the counter, you can't make a reservation, and (unusual for Paris) you can't smoke, none of which has kept it from having a perpetual queue. And, though Robuchon conceived of the Ateliers as an alternative to haute cuisine, in 2006 it was awarded its first Michelin star.

BALTHAZAR, NEW YORK

Now that faux French brasseries have proliferated like mushrooms in a rainy autumn, it's a bit difficult to appreciate just what a sensation Keith McNally's Balthazar caused when it first opened. Instead of attempting a chic *froideur,* it opted for nostalgia and succeeded. Its single-mindedly Old World decor—the artfully cracked tiles, large mirrors, and dented zinc bar could have been plucked from **Manet**'s *A Bar at the Folies-Bergères*—rather than making it feel phony, encouraged patrons to treat it more casually than they would a prissier establishment; it was, in effect, already broken in. New Yorkers put their cynicism aside and clasped it to their bosoms. Within weeks, it had acquired the daylong, happy bustle that, a decade on, still feels cheerfully authentic. And all that well-loved charm? It's no longer a trompe l'oeil effect but a reality.

The food is typical hearty brasserie fare—oysters, escargots, steak au poivre, tarte tatin—with a few standouts, including crisp, salty brown *frites* that are the best in the city. But it's the atmosphere, a McNally specialty—Odeon, one of his earlier ventures, so captured the mood of New York in the '80s that it was pictured on the cover of the Bret Easton Ellis novel *Bright Lights, Big City*—that's made Balthazar an enduring hit. Everyone looks good in the butter yellow light, and McNally made sure that this won't go unnoticed: The leather banquettes are high enough to be comfortable but low enough for unobstructed views all the way across the dining room. And the acoustics are just what they should be in a casual restaurant: Loud when you walk in, but quiet at the tables.

Getting a reservation for dinner can be difficult, but the best time to visit Balthazar is actually in the morning, for breakfast. From the smell of freshly baked croissants to the crisp linen, it's an especially civilized way to start the day.

DAVÉ, PARIS

Though it's in Paris, one of the world's great restaurant cities, no one comes to Davé for the food, which is Chinese and perfectly fine. Or the decor, which runs to lots of deep red and a disdain for lighting. The clientele, which consists almost exclusively of writers, rock stars, actors, directors, and fashionistas, come because they can. Booking a table is next to impossible, and if you're so brazen (or deluded) as to just show up, you'll find a *complet* sign on the door. If, however, as you stood on the pavement wondering where to try next, **Anna Wintour**, **Karl Lagerfeld**, Leonardo Di Caprio, or David Bowie were to be driven up, they'd be whisked inside. There may not be any discernible velvet rope, but Davé is more of a club than a restaurant, and only those who are on cheek-kissing terms with owner Davé Cheung get in.

Davé, as he is known to everyone, was born in Hong Kong but moved to Paris with his family when he was a teenager. He opened his restaurant in 1982, near the Jardins des Tuileries, one of the venues for Paris's fashion week (Davé moved to its present spot in 2002). **Helmut Newton** was one of his first customers, and, as the old shampoo commercial had it, he told two friends and they told two friends, and, voilà, a fashion cafeteria, with all the high-school rivalry that that suggests, was born. The restaurant has no menus; instead Davé hovers solicitously and suggests dishes.

Prices, which he considers vulgar, aren't alluded to until the table has been cleared and the bill is presented. It can be surprisingly high, but that doesn't bother anyone who eats here. Anyway, they're paying for something far more precious than a meal. As Davé once explained, "My job is to make fabulous people feel fabulous."

EL BULLI, GIRONA, SPAIN

Ask a food critic who the best chef in the world is and they'll probably answer Ferran Adrià. Though "chef" might not be quite the right word for it. While he's certainly a cook, he's also an artist, an alchemist, and a philosopher. His three-star Michelin restaurant, El Bulli, on the Costa Brava in Spain, a two-and-a-half-hour drive from Barcelona, is not a place you go to have a perfectly grilled steak. Even if the menu describes a dish as a perfectly grilled steak, it won't arrive on your plate looking anything like what you'd expect a perfectly grilled steak to look like. It may be liquefied, rendered into foam (the foam craze that swept restaurants a few years ago can be traced to Adrià's kitchen), or otherwise deconstructed, and it will probably be served in a dessert spoon or some other unlikely vessel.

Take one of his signature dishes, an interpretation of the classic tortilla Española, a sort of potato frittata. He begins by reducing it to its three main ingredients—eggs, potatoes, and onions—then treats each of these as a separate dish: The sliced potatoes become potato foam, the onions are reduced to a puree, and the eggs are whipped into a light custard. These elements are layered, topped with fried potato crumbs, and served in a sherry glass. Sounds mad, yes, but as you spoon up the layers, you get the taste experience of the best tortilla Española you've ever eaten, distilled into its purest form. It's a heady experience.

It's also one that keeps El Bulli, a restaurant that is essentially in the middle of nowhere, flooded with requests for dinner—more than four hundred for every table, almost all of them from people who have to travel thousands of miles to get there. It's a trick only the greatest chef in the world could pull off.

THE FAT DUCK, BRAY, BERKSHIRE, ENGLAND

That Britain, the land of beans on toast and fry-ups, is now a gastronomic capital is not lost on ironists. Nor is the fact that Heston Blumenthal, the self-taught chef at the helm of The Fat Duck, a former village pub that's now considered one of the top five restaurants in the world, has built his reputation on subverting these questionable dishes and turning them into epicurean triumphs. Bacon-and-egg ice cream (which, in a nice tongue-in-cheek gesture, is served with tea jelly), sardine-on-toast sorbet, and snail porridge are among the items you'll find on the menu there. Unappetizing as they may sound, all have been lavished with praise by Blumenthal's fellow *cuisiniers* and the many diners who flock to the small town of Bray to tuck in (the otherwise unassuming Bray is quite a gourmet destination: It's also home to The Waterside Inn, another much-vaunted restaurant).

Nursery food isn't all Blumenthal serves—poached breast of pigeon and leather, oak, and tobacco chocolates are also served at The Fat Duck—but he does take a keen delight in re-creating the childhood experience of sampling things for the first time. Taste and memory, along with an abiding interest in the way cooking transforms ingredients, are what motivate him. While other chefs try to dazzle you with their genius for combining flavors or their flair for innovation, Blumenthal is a sort of Proust of the saucepans, ever in search of new madeleines.

But he probably wouldn't put it in such highfalutin terms—Blumenthal believes food should be fun, a philosophy that's reflected in the atmosphere at his restaurant, which, while undoubtedly professional, is also casual and cheery. A night at The Fat Duck may not be a standard three-star experience, but it's probably far more memorable.

THE FRENCH LAUNDRY, YOUNTVILLE, CALIFORNIA

It's hard to decide what is the best time of day to dine at The French Laundry, which, as the name suggests, was once a French laundry. Lunch, when you can best appreciate the drive through the sun-dappled vineyards of the Napa Valley and the restaurant's fragrant rose and herb gardens? Or dinner, when the century-old stone cottage glows with golden candlelight? Both are appealing, but the decision probably won't be yours to make. The restaurant is booked two months in advance, and prospective diners tend to grab the first available table. The inconvenience of all this fades, however, when you sit down to begin one of Thomas Keller's nine-course, four-hour tasting menus (you can order à la carte, but Keller and his staff feel strongly that you don't get the full French Laundry experience if you do).

Though nine courses, with wine to accompany each, sound like more than it's possible to eat at a single sitting, Keller makes each one just a few bites in size, a trick he's repeated at his almost-as-celebrated restaurant in New York, Per Se. The idea is to sample as many flavors on the contemporary American-meets-traditional-French menu as possible. Though the offerings change daily, sample dishes include such meetings of lowbrow American and highbrow French influences as a soft-shell crab sandwich that's made with confit of tomato and served on toasted brioche and a salad that mixes watermelon-rind pickles with Niçoise olives.

All in all, eating chez Keller is a sensual extravaganza of an undertaking, one that impresses even the pickiest critics of American food: the French. As a critic for the Parisian newspaper *Le Monde* put it, "Is it possible that the best French restaurant is not in France?"

JEAN GEORGES, NEW YORK

In the second volume of Douglas Adams's sci-fi satire *The Hitchhiker's Guide to the Galaxy, The Restaurant at the End of the Universe*, Milliways, the eatery of the title, has huge windows from which patrons can, every evening, watch the universe explode as they dine on various delicacies. It's an experience that's brought to mind at Jean Georges, which has huge windows that overlook Central Park and food that twines Thai flavors with the traditions of French haute cuisine, a union that made chef Jean-Georges Vongerichten famous. The sky and the trees remain after you've polished off your foie gras with caramel sauce, turbot with Château-Chalon sauce, and roasted apricot tart, but, like the diners at Milliways, you're not really the same. Vongerichten has succeeded in completely reconfiguring fine dining, and his mellifluous meals linger in the taste buds and the memory.

Jean Georges, which holds three Michelin stars and four from *The New York Times* (the highest honor each publication gives), is one of sixteen restaurants in Vongerichten's global empire, but he still finds time to make regular appearances in its kitchen, a move that ensures that, ten years after it first opened, the food is as delicious as ever. In the dining room, the austere beige and white decor and the attentive staff—most dishes are finished at the table by the waiters, the better to show off their aromas and flavors—continue the effort to keep the focus on the food and the adventure of eating it.

The adventure doesn't come cheap, but lunch at Jean Georges (when the room feels much friendlier than it does by lamplight) is one of New York's great bargains.

PIERRE GAGNAIRE, PARIS

If traditional haute cuisine is a symphony, then Pierre Gagnaire's adventurous explorations into taste, texture, and color are improvisational jazz. The iconoclastic Gagnaire's riffs on French cooking go off on tangents that haven't always sat well with the buttoned-up food establishment—his first restaurant, near Lyon, went bankrupt despite its three Michelin stars. But he's reclaimed his Michelin standing and is riding high with his self-titled restaurant in the Hotel Balzac, which is routinely named one of the best in the world (as are Sketch, his restaurant/tearoom/gallery in London, and the more recent Pierre, in Hong Kong).

The elegant dining room, with its dove gray walls, heavy padded chairs, and honey-colored wood, is conventionally sedate, but that's just a foil for the anything-but-conventional or sedate food. Gagnaire strives to surprise his diners with unusual and intriguing combinations. He's especially fond of dabbling in sour and bitter tastes, which don't get much play in the French repertoire, and he likes to experiment with the way food feels in the mouth, juxtaposing, for example, smoothness and crunchiness where you'd least expect it. Complicated-sounding dishes like capon stuffed with almond paste, onion marmalade, and cherries require a spirit of adventure—Gagnaire is the first to acknowledge that his experiments don't always work—but if you're willing to go along with him, the rewards can be spectacular. In any case, the menu changes regularly, so anything that doesn't fly is soon replaced.

If you can't get into Pierre Gagnaire, Gaya, his Left Bank seafood restaurant, is both more accessible and far cheaper.

THE RIVER CAFÉ, LONDON

Though London has many great restaurants, few can claim the affection with which the twenty-year-old River Café is regarded. Located on a previously unvisited and rather bleak swath of the Thames in Hammersmith, it specializes in a sophisticated interpretation of home-style Italian peasant food, the kind that's built on perfectly fresh ingredients and a light and loving hand in the kitchen. It has also spawned dozens of imitators and numerous cookbooks, and functioned as something of a culinary university: Jamie Oliver, a.k.a. the Naked Chef, got his start here, as did April Bloomfield, who now hangs her apron at the Spotted Pig in Manhattan.

The restaurant was opened by Rose Gray, an Englishwoman, and Ruth Rogers, an American, neither of whom had any previous experience as professional chefs. But when Ruth's Florence-born husband, the celebrated architect **Richard Rogers**, opened his office in a complex that had space for a restaurant and wanted a good place to go for lunch, they decided to take their mutual love of Italian food and start a business. Richard transformed what had been a cavernous warehouse into a warm, inviting space with an open kitchen and a wood-burning oven, and they got to work perfecting dishes like Tuscan bread salad and pasta with zucchini and mint, and, within a few years, the River Café was being touted as the best Italian restaurant in Europe. It's now one of the British capital's landmarks, and despite the steep prices (nothing peasantlike about those), it's constantly full.

London is certainly not Florence and by no stretch of the imagination is the Thames the Arno. But on a gray English day, the sunny, simple food at The River Café is the next best thing to being in Tuscany.

TETSUYA'S, SYDNEY, AUSTRALIA

Not many cities can boast the kind of restaurant culture Sydney has produced in the past fifteen years. From its coffee snobbery to its obsession with fresh produce, this is a place that takes its food seriously. Restaurateurs are held to a high standard, and everyone has an opinion on what the city's best eatery is. For many, that's Tetsuya's, where Japanese-born chef Tetsuya Wakuda's flawless mingling of top-notch local ingredients, Japanese techniques, and European traditions has brought him—and, by extension, Australian cuisine—international acclaim.

Tets', as it's known locally, is a sprawling space in the center of town, decorated in spare Zen-chic style with bonsai trees, contemporary art, and indoor waterfalls—eating here is like dining in a tranquil Japanese garden. The twelve-course, seafood-heavy tasting menu (if that sounds daunting, lunch is a mere eight courses) is constantly evolving, but there are a few standards, such as Wakuda's signature *kombu*-sprinkled ocean trout served with unpasteurized ocean trout roe, a dish that's been known to make even hardened restaurant critics sigh with delight. But Wakuda is too much of a perfectionist to rest on his laurels; even this frequently requested item is under constant scrutiny, showing some subtle evolution each time it returns to the menu. He's also renowned for his slow-roasted rack of lamb with miso and blue cheese, a combination that sounds strange but offers a seamless blending of East and West, and his Asian-accented French desserts, such as an orange, honey, and black pepper sorbet that's served as the precursor to a blue-cheese *bavarois*.

CHEFS TO KNOW ABOUT

Despite prominently featuring offal on the menu at his string of restaurants in New York and Las Vegas, **Mario Batali**, the Italian American chef/restaurateur/TV host with the Falstaffian proportions, has managed to make Americans look at Italian food in a new light. **Paul Bocuse**, the main originator of nouvelle cuisine in the early 1970s, was one of the first chefs to emerge from the kitchen and into the public eye. Lyon-born **Daniel Boulud** is the chef and owner of New York's Daniel, which holds two Michelin stars and has been called the best place to have French food outside of France. **Alain Ducasse** is the only chef in the world to have been awarded three stars in three different countries by the Michelin Guide for his restaurants in Paris, Monaco, and New York (now closed). Tough Scot **Gordon Ramsay** is known for his temper and the three Michelin stars he's been awarded for Gordon Ramsay at Royal Hospital Road in London, one of his many restaurants. He's now set his sights on success in the U.S. **Joël Robuchon** is credited with leading the French away from nouvelle cuisine and back to the simpler pleasures of old-fashioned bourgeois dishes, such as *pomme purée*. Though he's from the German-accented Alsace region of France, **Jean-Georges Vongerichten**'s fame stems from his innovative fusion of Thai and French cuisine, which is served at his award-winning restaurants in the U.S., the U.K., and the Far East, the most famous of which is **Jean Georges**, winner of three Michelin stars.

PRONUNCIATION GUIDE

Paul Bocuse:
PAUL bow-COOZ

Daniel Boulud:
dan-YELL boo-LOO

WHAT YOU NEED TO KNOW ABOUT WINE

THOUGH IT'S BEYOND the scope of this book to provide an encyclopedic guide to vineyards and vintages, the basics of wine are actually fairly straightforward. There are other grapes, of course, but master the characteristics of these basic reds and whites and you'll be able to order wine with confidence.

WHITE WINE

In the way that spring is easier than winter, white wine is often easier than red. It's cleaner tasting than red and best served chilled. White wine is elegant. It evokes crisp, clean images, such as freshly mowed grass or tall glasses of lemon sherbet. Sweeter whites have undertones of vanilla, while drier (i.e., less sweet) ones tend to have a hint of tartness, as though you've just eaten a slice of grapefruit. If red wine is a black cocktail dress, white wine is a cream-colored trench coat.

THE GRAPES:

CHARDONNAY   Chardonnay is the wine version of vanilla ice cream: sweet, easy to drink, and inoffensive. And just like anything vanilla, it's often frowned on by connoisseurs, who find it over-oaked (oak barrels are what give wine its vanilla or butterscotch taste; unscrupulous winemakers use oak to hide the flavor of inferior grapes) and boring. Chardonnay is one of the most widely grown grapes in the world, found everywhere from France to Australia to California. As with anything that's produced in such vast quantities, mediocrity is a problem. But good Chardonnays can be lovely. White Burgundy, for example, which is almost always made entirely from Chardonnay grapes, is highly regarded for its honeyed, apple-scented earthiness. In general, Chardonnays grown in warmer climates, especially those originating in California, are sweeter and fuller-bodied, while the ones grown in more temperate areas, such as France, have a subtler bouquet.

> **PRONUNCIATION GUIDE**
>
> **Chardonnay:**
> **shar-doh-NAY**

SAUVIGNON BLANC   The Sauvignon Blanc grape has a bite to it. It's most commonly described as smelling of grass, though its tangy green scent is also suggestive of mint or lemongrass or some other sharp-tasting herb. As always with wine, its *terroir*, a French term that denotes the singular personality given to a wine by the soil and weather in which its grapes were grown, is key. Sauvignon Blancs from California, which has higher temperatures than much of the rest of the winemaking world, tend to be slightly bland—and because winemakers there use oak barrels, it's sweeter. Wines from the Loire Valley, on the other hand, including bone-dry Sancerres and Pouilly-Fumés, have more of a citrus kick. In Bordeaux, another Sauvignon Blanc growing

> **PRONUNCIATION GUIDE**
>
> **Sauvignon Blanc:**
> **so-vee-NYOHN blahn**
> **Terroir:**
> **tehr-WAHR**

region of France, it's blended with the more robust Sémillon grape to make mellow white Bordeaux. But at the moment, the most exciting Sauvignon Blancs come from New Zealand, where intense sunshine and a relatively cool climate result in wines that are both heady and refined.

PINOT GRIS   At its best, Pinot Gris is a crisp, dry wine with an agreeably clean, slightly nutty finish. This dark-skinned grape (*gris* means gray in French) is grown in Alsace and in Oregon, but the most widely known Pinot Gris is actually Pinot Grigio, its northern Italian cousin. That's too bad, because Pinot Grigio is all too often a thin, underflavored disappointment. It's not that Italy doesn't produce some fine Pinot Grigios—those originating in Friuli and Trentino-Alto Adige are particularly worth seeking out—but the underwhelming variety is far more common, especially in restaurants with limited wine lists. However, it's the rich clay soil and abundant sunshine of northern Alsace that make the best Tokay-Pinot Gris, as it's known there. Alsatian Pinot Gris is rich and complex, and gets more buttery as it ages. Oregon's Pinot Gris are zestier, as are some of the varieties grown in California's Napa Valley.

> **PRONUNCIATION GUIDE**
>
> **Pinot Grigio:**
> **PEE-no GREE-zhee-oh**
> **Pinot Gris:**
> **PEE-no GREE**

RED WINE

Red wine is rich, complex, earthy. At its best, it bursts with the sort of flavors associated with pure pleasure: ripe berries, dark chocolate, truffles, bouquets of roses. In fashion terms, red wine is a black velvet dress—or a well-worn leather jacket. It's red lipstick and high heels, worn with jeans or to the opera. In general, red wines are purple-y when they're young, ruby red when they've reached a certain age, and tinged with gold when they're mature.

THE GRAPES:

CABERNET SAUVIGNON   This small, thick-skinned, blue-black grape is the king of the wine world. It grows pretty much any-where, as long as it's not too cool, and produces big-tasting, full-bodied wines that are high in tannin, which is the substance in red wine that gives it its firm, rather astringent taste. Tan-nin is found in grape skins, which are fermented along with the grape in the production of red wine. White wine isn't fer-mented with the skins, so it has no tannin; this is the chief difference between red and white wine. Cabernet Sauvignon is used to make red Bordeaux, one of the finest wines in the world, and it's an integral part of the Super Tuscans. It's also the grape that kicked off the Cali-fornia wine boom. Cabernet Sauvignon has an intense cassis flavor, with an underlying spiciness. New World Cabernet Sauvignons are meant to be enjoyed straightaway, and tend to be less complex than their Old World cousins, which are best savored after a few years.

> **PRONUNCIATION GUIDE**
>
> **Cabernet Sauvignon:**
> **ka-ber-NAY so-vee-NYOHN**

MERLOT   Merlot is to red wine what **Chardonnay** is to white—the fail-safe, default order for the casual imbiber. And, as with Char-donnay, that means that there are an awful lot of watered-down, insipid bottles of it out there; it's not a good bargain-bin choice. But a good Merlot is an opulent, plummy, sensuous drink, perfect for sipping on a winter's evening. Because it has less tannin than **Cabernet Sauvignon**, some people find it easier to like. Conversely, winemakers often feel that it's a bit too soft and will some-times blend it with that bitterer grape to make a more multilayered wine. In Bordeaux, where Mer-lot grapes are planted extensively, it's most often used to moderate the bite of Cabernet Sauvignon and is an essential component in the region's famous red Bordeaux. It's also grown in California, Washing-ton, Italy, and Australia. But some of the best and most affordable Merlots come from Chile.

> **PRONUNCIATION GUIDE**
>
> **Merlot:**
> **mer-LOH**

PINOT NOIR   Compared with easy-growing **Cabernet Sauvignon**, thin-skinned Pinot Noir is the problematic adolescent of the wine world, requiring elaborate care and attention but not always rewarding its growers with the results they'd hoped for. Producing Pinot Noir is a labor of love, not a business decision. Consequently, to get a good bottle, you have to pay upward of twenty dollars. But if you're willing to invest the money, you may find yourself drinking one of the most remarkable wines you've ever sampled. Pinot Noir has a fragrant, cherry-and-smoke

> **PRONUNCIATION GUIDE**
>
> **Pinot Noir:**
> **PEE-noh NWAHR**

bouquet, a satin-smooth body, and a notable lack of mouth-drying tannins. It's nuanced and fairly intense, yet remarkably easy to drink. It's even nice to look at, with a clear, light strawberry color. Pinot Noir's prototype is red Burgundy, another maddeningly inconsistent wine. But red Burgundy is a more robust, bawdy wine than its New World cousin, and is often drunk when it's mature, while Pinot Noir is best enjoyed young.

THE CHAMPAGNE HOUSES

Despite its alarmingly English-seeming name, **Bollinger** is a high-quality house based in the Champagne region of France, where the only wines that can be called Champagne-with-a-capital-*C* are made. It's the preferred drink of James Bond, for what that's worth. The LVMH-owned house of **Krug** (the luxury goods giant also owns Moët et Chandon and Veuve Clicquot), founded in 1843 by Jean-Joseph Krug, doesn't make bubbly for the entry-level sipper. Its rarefied *prestige cuvées* are at the top end of the market, with some varieties yielding only one thousand cases a season. **Louis Roederer**, the maker of the hip-hop-approved Cristal, is also rarefied—this premium Champagne was originally made for Czar Alexander II of Russia, who wanted something that would really wow his dinner guests. **Perrier-Jouët**, with its pretty art nouveau bottles, was founded in 1811, and makes a frothy, light-bodied wine that's easy to sip. **Moët et Chandon** is the largest Champagne producer in the world and was allegedly a favorite of Napoleon's. It's a good, reliable brand with a medium body at the not-too-pricey (for Champagne, anyway) end of the market. As is **Veuve Clicquot**, which means the widow Clicquot. The full-bodied Champagnes from this house make a perennially pleasing hostess gift.

PRONUNCIATION GUIDE

Bollinger: bow-lahn-ZHAY

Krug: KREWG

Louis Roederer: loo-WEE roe-duh-REHR

Moët et Chandon: moe-EHT AY shan-DOH

Perrier-Jouët: PEH-ree-ay zhew-EH

Veuve Clicquot: VUHV klee-KOH

FIVE COCKTAILS
TO ORDER

EVEN WHEN A CERTAIN television series about sex and shoes and New York City was on the air, the Cosmopolitan had already had its moment on the bar. There are far more chic cocktails to order, such as any of these.

NB: Cocktail connoisseurs feel strongly about shaking versus stirring. Drinks made of pure alcohol should be stirred, not shaken, while drinks made with nonalcoholic mixers should be shaken. And cracked or shaved ice is preferable to cubes.

FRENCH 75

This World War I–era cocktail is named for a gun, not a kiss.

> 1 ounce gin
> ¼ ounce lemon juice
> ⅛ ounce simple syrup
> 5 ounces chilled Champagne

Shake gin, lemon juice, and simple syrup with ice; strain into a Champagne flute, and top with Champagne. Can also be made with cognac instead of gin.

MANHATTAN

The Manhattan was first served at New York's Manhattan Club in 1876, at a banquet hosted by Lady Randolph Churchill (Winston's mother) for the presidential candidate Samuel Tilden.

> 2 ounces whiskey
> 2 ounces sweet vermouth
> Dash Angostura bitters

Fill a cocktail shaker one-quarter full of ice, then add all ingredients, and shake or stir well. Strain into a martini glass. Garnish with a maraschino cherry.

MARTINI

This all-time classic was described by writer and boozehound H. L. Mencken as "the only American invention as perfect as the sonnet." Incidentally, all the blather about "just showing the vermouth bottle to the gin" started after Prohibition ended. Before that, vermouth was used more liberally, to hide the sometimes-questionable taste of bathtub gin.

> 2 ounces gin
> 2 drops dry vermouth (the less vermouth you use, the drier the martini)

Combine all ingredients in a shaker with ice and strain into a chilled martini glass (shaking a martini results in a colder, albeit weaker drink). Garnish with an olive.

NEGRONI

The Negroni was named for Count Camillo Negroni, who in the early 1920s asked a Florence bartender to add gin to this favorite tipple, the Americano.

1 ounce gin
¾ ounce sweet vermouth
1 ounce Campari

Shake all ingredients in a shaker with ice and strain into a chilled martini glass. Garnish with a twist of lemon. This can also be served on the rocks in a lowball glass.

SIDECAR

This popular Jazz Age drink was supposedly invented by an American officer in Paris during World War I, and named for the motorcycle sidecar he was driven around in.

1½ ounces brandy
½ ounce Triple Sec
½ ounce lemon juice

Combine all ingredients in a shaker filled with ice, shake well, and strain into a chilled martini glass.

EPILOGUE

AS PROMISED in the introduction, there's no exam at the end of *In the Know*. You've probably concluded on your own that cool isn't something you can be quizzed about—it's too hazy, free-flowing a quality to stand up to that kind of scrutiny. Cool is something you recognize when you see it. It's the recognition that's the crucial thing. It comes from being aware of what to look for, and it's these scattered clues—the literary references, the artistic movements, the design statements—that *In the Know* is really about. Now that you're familiar with them, you can make your own call on what's cool.

INDEX